R I S E

a reformer's handbook for the
SEVEN MOUNTAINS

Contents

CHAPTER ONE   Live Your Purpose 5

CHAPTER TWO   How to Use the Reformer's Handbook 21

CHAPTER THREE   The Mountain of Media 33

CHAPTER FOUR   The Mountain of Family 47

CHAPTER FIVE   The Mountain of Arts & Entertainment 61

CHAPTER SIX   The Mountain of Economy 75

CHAPTER SEVEN   The Mountain of Religion 89

CHAPTER EIGHT   The Mountain of Education 103

CHAPTER NINE   The Mountain of Government 117

CHAPTER TEN   The Rising Reformers 129

Join the RISE Global Community 135

Appendix:

- Overcoming End-Times-Itis 139
- RISE Quick Reference Chart 146
- Other Recommended Resources 148

CHAPTER ONE

Live Your Purpose

Every human has an innate sense that we were born for more than just survival. We are wired to instinctively believe that we each have a purpose in life and a unique role to play. Most of us live without purpose—either stuck in survival mode, feeling too distracted or overwhelmed to find our true purpose, or stuck in achieving accomplishments that are far less than what God desires for us. Our lack of purpose not only affects us individually, but also collectively as a society. Society itself experiences far less than what God has destined for us. Are you ready to do something about it? Are you ready to live your purpose?

RISE, which stands for Reformers Influencing Society Everyday, is a movement of reformers who have fully connected to their purpose. They lead with love, are motivated by hope, and are infused with faith to see heaven come to earth through tangible solutions for individuals, cities, and nations. They're a part of a global community that exists beyond the four walls of a church to awaken, equip, and connect those who believe that God not only loves and cares about all of humanity, but also desires to display His love, kindness, and goodness through His sons and daughters in all areas of culture.

Every nation has seven primary areas of culture, or mountains, that were meant to be the format, or the context, in which we receive God's ever-increasing kingdom: Media, Family, Arts & Entertainment, Economy, Religion, Education, and Government.

God is brilliant and relatable in the way He has given us the areas of our lives that we daily engage with, connect with, and care the most about (the seven areas of culture) as a framework to receive His kingdom and the essence of who He is on earth. God's kingdom involves God's better way of doing everything and the solving of every problem. God's essence is His love. In the simplest way to describe Him—He is love. Our lives are ultimately a journey to discover and understand what love looks like—what God as love looks like in each of these areas of culture—as His kingdom, His better ways and solutions are coming to earth. Because there's no fear in love and perfect love casts out all fear, we will know that the kingdom has fully come, and that God is properly being displayed in each area of culture when we're able to experience that area of culture and our conclusive takeaway is, "I felt loved."

Where love is truly present we are instinctively wired to believe that there is a God and He cares about us.

> *What comes into our mind when we think about God*
> *is the most important thing about us.* — *A. W. Tozer*

To the degree we have a limited or diminished perspective of who God is, to that degree we ourselves are limited and diminished in our purpose and in life in general. The less we have known of God, the less we will access and reveal of Him. We must bring solutions into these seven structures of society in a way that reflects who God is and how He loves us.

Reformers are those who are ready to walk in their purpose outside of the four walls of the church. A reformer is focused, hopeful, and ready to see change. They are waging war on religion and on the mindsets that have caused God's reputation on earth to be less than He really is. These reformers love radically without religion's agenda and believe the goodness of God can be expressed in every area of culture.

RISE is the answer for lovers of Jesus who know they were created to change the world but haven't known exactly what that looks like in real life. God desires to partner with His sons and daughters to display the truth of not just *who* He is, but *how* He is in the earth and to reform every broken system in the seven mountains of culture. If you're fully convinced that the real God loves the world and has solutions for every problem that exists in society, then RISE is for you.

RISE: A Reformer's Handbook for the Seven Mountains is a condensed overview of the most important things a reformer needs to understand in order to effectively impact the areas of culture they have influence and passion for changing. Either by reading this handbook and/or completing the RISE Course online, you're qualified to join the RISE Global Community.

For more details:
www.RESTORE7.org

ESSENTIALS FOR REFORMERS

The following are seven essential truths every reformer must understand in order to fulfill their purpose to know God and make Him known in the areas of culture they are called to impact:

1. A REFORMER MUST UNDERSTAND THE SEVEN MOUNTAIN MANDATE: FILL THE EARTH WITH THE KNOWLEDGE OF THE GLORY OF GOD

A mandate is a command or an authorization given by a political electorate to its representatives. In the context of the seven mountains, the mandate we were given by God is to fill the earth with the knowledge of the glory of God as His representatives, ones who were made in His image. It is both our privilege and our assignment. God Himself described a picture of our guaranteed end-game like this:

> *"The earth will be filled with the **knowledge of the glory of God**,*
> *as the waters cover the sea."*
> ***Habakkuk 2:14***

The knowledge of God is the understanding of not only *who* He is, but also *how* He is, or what He's like. The glory of God is His essence—what He's really like, what motivates Him, and what is uniquely Him. In the Old Testament Moses asked to see God's glory, and in response God caused all His goodness to pass before him. In this profound experience Moses had, we understand that a major part of the glory of God is simply how good He is. So, when we talk about the knowledge of the glory of God filling the earth, we are basically saying that at some point everyone will have access to the understanding of who God is, what He's really like, and how good He is.

Presently, every area of culture is being used by the enemy to perpetuate lies about who God is and who we are to Him. As reformers rise on the mountains of culture, the lies will be demolished and replaced with irrefutable proof that there is a God, He loves and cares for us, and He has solutions for all our individual and collective problems. God cares about every aspect of culture and everything that affects us, not just our souls for eternity. The saving knowledge of God is just one aspect of the knowledge of God that is available for receiving and displaying. Within each of the seven mountains, our assignment is to see

_____
_____
_____
_____
_____
_____
_____
_____
_____
_____
_____
_____
_____
_____
_____
_____
_____
_____
_____
_____
_____
_____
_____
_____
_____

and know God in an expanded way and then re-image Him in society. Because God's image is not just male, God's fullness can only be properly represented in culture when both male and female voices, perspectives, and influence are equally valued and implemented.

The specific term "mountain" comes from Revelation 17:9, "Here is the mind which has wisdom: The seven heads are seven mountains on which the woman sits." Earlier in that same chapter it refers to the woman as Babylon or the harlot who we understand to represent Satan, his principalities, and their demonic system that comes against the seven mountains of culture in every nation with a seven-pronged attack. Proverbs 9:1-3 says, "Wisdom has built her house, she has hewn out her seven pillars...and cries out from the high places of the city." Wisdom is a term for the Holy Spirit, who is building the kingdom of God on earth on the seven pillars, or mountains, of society.

In our effort to understand the mandate to fill the earth with the knowledge of God, we need to understand that we were born into a war zone with a very real enemy—and the enemy isn't broken or deceived people nor the broken systems of culture. Satan is the enemy. He deceived Adam and Eve by tempting them to exchange their intimate knowledge of God for another knowledge. When they ate of the tree of the knowledge of good and evil, they, like us, gained the ability to look at something or someone (at God) and question whether He's good or evil—whether His heart towards us is good or evil. The Serpent conspired with an argument against God's reputation and ever since that day we have been expert doubters of God, lacking trust in and understanding of the One who loves us perfectly.

That initial battle is replayed daily all across the planet through every circumstance we go through, and it has led to systems and mountains of society being built around lies about God. Satan leveraged our propensity to view the knowledge of God, and ultimately His goodness, through every circumstance of our life. He convinced us as humanity to construct systems in every area of culture that are our best ways rather than God's best ways—because we believe, if He exists, that He certainly doesn't care enough about us to know what's best for us. So, we build ways of taking care of ourselves based on lies about God. Systems built on lies about God will always be a place for a stronghold of the enemy. Our assignment is to know God so well that we recognize the foundation of each lie and build upon the truth of who He is instead. **The war is all about God being properly known the way He was originally intended to be known in each area of culture.**

2 Corinthians 10:4-5 tells us, "The weapons of our warfare are not carnal but mighty for the pulling down of strongholds. Casting down arguments and every high thing that exalts itself against the knowledge of God..." Our battle is a battle of knowledge. Satan has no actual power to harm God. He is limited to injuring God by how he distorts the image of God to all His sons and daughters. He plans and creates lies and arguments against the correct reputation or perspective of God and because Satan has no real power of his own, he is empowered by those he's able to deceive. His lies and arguments then become a stronghold that holds back entire people groups, entire cities, and entire nations. This is how he holds sway in each of the seven mountains. His stronghold is an argument or a mentality that doesn't acknowledge God. If we understand that Satan's stronghold or fortress is nothing but a deceived and false argument or idea about God, then we understand that the way to ultimately eliminate his position of stronghold is to bring the true and correct knowledge of God that overthrows the lie. The root problem is that there's a lie about God that hasn't been replaced with the truth. The battle is over the knowledge of God—the correct reputation of our Father. When we contend for the restoration of our God's reputation, we're heading for the front lines of spiritual warfare.

Paul, in Ephesians 1:17-18, prayed that God would "give you the spirit of wisdom and revelation in the knowledge of Him, that the eyes of your understanding being enlightened; that you may know what is the hope of His calling; what are the riches of the glory of His inheritance in the saints and what is the exceeding greatness of His power towards us who believe, according to the working of His mighty power." God wants to be revealed through His enlightened sons and daughters. An expanded knowledge of God is mighty, mighty power because, when it's reflected into society, it pulls down the stronghold of Satan in that area of culture. We are to prioritize the knowledge of the glory of God above every other knowledge that exists.

2. A REFORMER MUST UNDERSTAND HOW AUTHORITY OVER THE SEVEN MOUNTAINS WAS LOST AND REGAINED

"For the Son of Man came to save that which was lost."
Matthew 18:11

When Adam and Eve sinned, they were disconnected from God's original plan for all His sons and daughters. They lost authority—the privileged position and responsibility of dominion/stewardship in the earth. From that time until Jesus regained it, humanity lost authority specifically over the seven mountains, or foundations of power, that were meant to express who God is in the earth. Through their sin Satan gained legal authority to distort the "face" of God on earth—our correct perception of Him and His heart towards us.

In Matthew 4, known as the Temptation of Christ, we're told that the devil took Jesus up on a high mountain and showed Him all the kingdoms of the world and their authority. He told Jesus that he would give Him all the kingdoms if Jesus would bow down and worship him. The word kingdoms here means *basilea*, or foundations of power. The kingdoms Satan referred to aren't specifically nations, but rather the foundations of power upon which nations are built—the seven mountains of culture. Luke 4, an account of the same story, tells us that Satan reminded Jesus that he had been given authority and the glory of the kingdoms and could give it to whomever he wanted. Satan tempted Jesus with the one thing he knew Jesus had come to reclaim—the lost authority over the seven areas of culture that Jesus planned to give back to us.

Satan was offering Jesus a shortcut to what He knew Jesus was here to accomplish through His death and resurrection that had not yet taken place. Notice that Satan wasn't bartering with Jesus over the souls of people. It was about the kingdoms of power, which included the souls. Jesus came to save *that* which was lost, not simply *those* that were lost. From the time of Jesus' death, all jurisdiction was His and then He gave it to us. Therefore, all principalities, powers, and demons are illegally on the mountains of culture in every nation.

"Jesus said, 'All authority has been given to me in heaven and on earth. Go therefore and make disciples of all the nations.'"
Matthew 28:18-19

The Great Commission, given to us by Jesus after His death and resurrection, was to "make disciples of all nations." It was not to "make disciples of all souls." God is interested in the nations—a word mentioned over three hundred times in the Scriptures. Most of the Old Testament prophets prophesied to nations or cities; their blessings and/or curses were given on a citywide or nationwide basis. The nations themselves each have a destiny and an identity in the eyes of the Lord. He loves nations and He loves cities, as well as their unique cultural expressions. Jesus made it clear that He came first for "the lost house of Israel" (Matthew 15:24)—for a nation.

When He wept in Luke 13:34, His cry was for "Jerusalem, Jerusalem"—for a city. Haggai 2:7 calls Him the Desire of the Nations. Whether we understand it or not, He is jealous over entire countries. His zeal is to have them under the reign of our just and kind Father. That's the gospel of the kingdom.

3. A REFORMER MUST UNDERSTAND THE GOSPEL OF THE KINGDOM VS. THE GOSPEL OF SALVATION

In His very first public message, Jesus connected us to our kingdom purpose as He announced in Matthew 5:13-14, "You are the salt of the earth...you are the light of the world." When we understand, as Jesus' audience did, that salt is a valuable preservative which prevents food from rotting, we better understand our important role in society. Any area of culture that we don't bring the salt and light of God's better ways to will eventually rot. Our influence can only be effective if we aren't hidden and we actually show up in every area of culture. Jesus went on to explain that our light should be on a candlestick, which they all would have instantly connected to the visual of the seven-branched candlestick in the temple. The candlestick we are told to shine our light from represents the seven burning flames or spirits of God in the throne room that are described in Revelation 4. For every darkness that exists on planet earth there is a light, a fire from the heart of Who God is, that is ready to displace that darkness through reformers. We must begin connecting to that fire of Who He is and bring that in a practical way to society.

"This gospel of the kingdom will be preached in the whole world as a testimony to all nations, and then the end will come."
Matthew 24:14

NOTES

The gospel of the kingdom must be our focus, not the gospel of salvation. The gospel of the kingdom doesn't diminish the gospel of salvation, it includes it. When we preach the gospel of the kingdom like Jesus did, then we not only care about souls, we care about everything that affects humanity, because God does. As important as it is to want people to one day live in heaven, it is equally important to be aware that Jesus' very first message was more about trying to get heaven on earth than about trying to get people into heaven. In that same message, He said, "In this manner, therefore, pray: ...Your kingdom come. Your will be done on earth as it is in heaven" (Matthew 6:9–10). Somehow, we have become stuck with a narrative that prioritizes getting people prepared for heaven, yet Jesus came proclaiming a different priority—a priority of heaven coming down to earth. He didn't present the sinner's prayer in His first message but rather pleaded for partners in reforming society. Obviously, He also cared for people's eternal state, but the scope of the kingdom of God—His better way of doing everything—is broader than that.

Realistically, when we talk about "on earth as it is in heaven," we need to recognize that God doesn't have periodic meetings in heaven where He asks for every head to be bowed and leads people in the sinner's prayer. So, the kingdom coming to earth is not about salvations; it's about the functionality of the kingdom and the institutions of heaven. The kingdom is the rule and reign of heaven, and so the mission is to manifest the rule and reign of heaven on earth—to showcase heaven's better institutions. Heaven is not just a place filled with happy people, but a place filled with happy institutions. The seven mountains on earth also exist in heaven: media (communication), family (relationships), arts and entertainment (beauty and fun), economy (provision), religion (worship), education (learning), and government (we will reign with Him). These are the seven primary spheres or structures of society in every nation. Jesus' prayer was that heaven's model of these structures would come manifest "on earth as it is in heaven." This is absolutely going to happen, because Jesus' prayer will not go unanswered.

4. A REFORMER MUST UNDERSTAND INFLUENCE VS. DOMINIONISM

In our excitement over this new seven mountain paradigm and assignment, we may sometimes get a little carried away in how we express it. We have noticed that Christians tend to like to use language such as "I'm going to 'take' the Mountain of _____." Likewise, I have heard of a lot of aggressive conversation about how we Christians are "taking over"—and we also seem to have a significant fascination with the word dominion. So, before we embark on bringing reformation into the mountains of society, we will really have to exercise wisdom as we describe our missional narrative. Society is listening in, and we need to be aware that the attention they pay to us will only increase as we move forward. Humanity's dominion mandate from God is clear from the book of Genesis, but we must understand that none of the descriptions of dominion ever talk about it in regard to dominating our fellow human beings.

"God said, 'Let Us make man in Our image, according to Our likeness; let them have dominion over the fish of the sea, over the birds of the air, and over the cattle, over all the earth and over every creeping thing that creeps on the earth...Then God blessed them, and God said to them, 'Be fruitful and multiply; fill the earth and subdue it; have dominion over the fish of the sea, over the birds of the air, and over every living thing that moves on the earth.'" Genesis 1:26, 28

Dominion is clearly laid out as a partnership between God and man over all other forms of life or existence, including the demonic realm. Therefore, whenever we use the language of dominion, if we don't immediately follow up with an explanation about what that means exactly, then we leave a huge open door for controversy, criticism, and a backlash of fear. "Having dominion" is not about Christians ruling over non-Christians, and we should always be aware of that fact. The dominion mandate was about the sons and daughters of God—all of humanity—having dominion over fish, cattle, birds, and all the earth, including every creeping thing and every living thing. Those last two categories would qualify as potential descriptions of demonic forces and they must be the focus of the domination.

"We do not wrestle against flesh and blood [people],
but against principalities, against powers, against the rulers of the
darkness of this age [Satan and his demons] ...."
Ephesians 6:12

The purpose of "wrestling" is to gain domination over the demonic realm and the lies it promotes about God. The targets of our domination are Satan and demons, and we must make sure that we always understand that narrative and represent it correctly. The history of the world is rife with examples of attempted Christian domination over all other religions. For many, many centuries, there was a pervasive atmosphere of religious imposition, and most of us would not have done well living in that reality. One needs only to read about the period of the Holy Inquisition to understand how a dominion mandate can get way out of hand. The true dominion mandate is stewardship over the planet, and it is to be seen as an extension of our carrying the image of the One who created us. It is a mandate to express His heart of love through every area of culture—and when that is done His way, the earth will rejoice!

Influence, versus imposition, happens in an atmosphere of freedom. The great value of influence is that it occurs under free will. Luke 2:52 says, "Jesus increased in wisdom and stature, and in favor with God and men." Influence is the by-product of having favor. Favor is an irresistibility factor that often defies logic. True godly favor is that which comes by carrying a high measure of love. That high measure of love will manifest in actions that are attractive to people of goodwill and unattractive to people of devious intent. This must be our goal for how we desire to advance the kingdom of God: We must resist any and all impulses to impose upon the masses that which should be only a matter of conscience between man and God. May what we write, what we say, and how we say it begin to catch up with that important understanding. There is a beauty of freedom that outweighs the beauty of order. Again, the kingdom of God comes in freedom, and the order it brings is an inside-out order, not an outside-in order. We must watch how we use dominion terminology and make sure that we are at no time shifting toward order by means of imposition, nor even a hidden agenda or motive to impose. God has always had the power to do in a mere instant what He desires to accomplish. Yet He has chosen to endure the arduous process of winning over hearts and minds through love. As He is, so must we be in this world.

5. A REFORMER MUST UNDERSTAND THE END-TIMES NARRATIVE AND HAVE VALUE FOR OUR PLANET

Perhaps nothing has been more sabotaging to the Body of Christ's assignment to be salt and light and thus transforming society, then what we will call the virus of end-times-itis—a "condition" marked by the expectation of soon coming, end-of-world scenarios. End-times-itis involves believing that either the rapture, or Jesus' return, or a one world government, or the anti-Christ, or Armageddon or some whole list of cataclysmic judgments is right around the corner. This "virus" saps our resolve and allows fear to reign. It's so widespread among Christians of all denominations (and even among virtually all false religions), that many of you reading this right now might be taken aback at me pointing this out as an issue. Our goal is to provide some needed truth serum that will vaccinate you from succumbing to it.

This fascination with the end-times has been alive and well among Christians for almost 2,000 years. There hasn't been even one generation that wasn't preoccupied with it. It clearly explains why, despite Christians being the greatest majority on the planet, we have comparatively little influence. It's hard to "arise and shine" when you're secretly or not so secretly planning your exit strategy.

A proper understanding of the end-times, or correct narrative to live by, is important because, if you don't know the "movie script" you're a part of, you'll play the wrong role. God has given us a role and a script where His glory will fall on all the nations. When we have a misguided understanding of the end-times and don't know our role and the big-picture narrative, then we have a faulty foundation and lack of vision.

We hasten Jesus' return by living our purpose and fulfilling the assignment He has given us. He will continue to let generation after generation die—and won't return—until at least one generation gets the assignment and performs His will on Earth as it is in heaven. Acts 3: 21 tells us that Jesus is held in heaven "until the restoration of all things spoken of by the prophets." Until sons and daughters rise to fulfill the original mission of subduing the darkness that pervades the earth, Jesus is held in the heavens. He will not return until this is accomplished. You can pray for His return until you are blue in the face, but He's not coming back until someone finishes the assignment. He is sitting in intercession for us at the right hand of the Father until all His enemies are put under our feet. Once His enemies are crushed, every next level of good things which God has intended to take place here on Earth will occur.

Jesus will return to earth again and there will be a new earth and new Heaven. That does not mean this planet will be eradicated, but rather it will no longer be the way it is now. The new earth is not a different earth—but, just like we become new creatures when we receive Jesus, so too the earth will be upgraded when the new Jerusalem descends. There will be an extreme world makeover by God, through His children who so thoroughly know who He is that they will access His better ways of doing everything. They will care about what He cares about, all people and all nations, and display God as love in every area of culture.

Not only is a reformer's end-time view important, but our value of planet Earth is theologically important as well. Throughout the entire creation story of Genesis, we read over and over again, "And God saw that it was good," with every new thing He spoke into existence in the earth. God loves this earth that He created. He made it with intention and design as a mirrored representation of what is in Heaven. Earth should not be viewed by us as simply disposable. We know from scripture that the righteous inherit the earth and the meek will inherit the earth. Psalm 2:8 says, "Ask of Me, and I will give You the nations for Your inheritance, and the ends of the earth for Your possession." If the Earth is of little value and disposable, then why would He give it as an inheritance? How can we inherit it if He is going to destroy it? The Earth will be filled with the glory of God.

(For a much more extensive historical perspective on this topic, please read *Overcoming End-times-itis* in the Appendix section of this manual.)

6. A REFORMER MUST UNDERSTAND THE SIMPLICITY OF LIVING INTENTIONALLY

Living with intention requires living with an end purpose in mind and deliberately choosing to act out of your core values or beliefs towards that purpose, rather than react out of personal wounds and subsequent lies we have believed. Our lack of trust in God keeps us reacting as if He doesn't truly care for us and living like we have to figure out our own solutions to all the world's problems or just survive until we are rescued. Unless we are intentional with why we are here and what we ultimately want to accomplish, how will we fulfill our purpose, which is ultimately to know Him in all the ways He can be known here on earth?

When we first learn the vastness of the assignment God has invited us into, it can feel complicated and overwhelming. Reformers must remember that, first of all, God can do this with or without us. He chooses to partner with us because He is relational— He loves an excuse to connect with us and He wants us fully invested in the certain victory so that we will enjoy the celebration even more for all of eternity. He also wants us, in the midst of impacting culture while we juggle the mundane realities of life itself, to keep it simple. His kingdom is profound, yet simple. We like to use the following statement to help us daily live our purpose:

I LIVE...
TO KNOW THE REAL HIM,
TO MAKE THE REAL HIM KNOWN,
AND TO LEARN TO LOVE
AND BE LOVED.

You want to make God known and fill the earth with the knowledge of His glory? Then know Him personally and grow in the knowledge of God yourself every day. You want to learn how to love God, yourself, and others better? Then learn how to let yourself encounter the reality of God's love for you every day and you will overflow with it. We cannot give away what we don't have and if what we have is not love or a distorted perspective of what God truly cares about, then how can we ever show the world love and who the real God is? Each area of a nation's culture displays the reality of lies that its citizens have embraced about God and His ways of doing things—or a false perspective that He doesn't want to be involved at all. Ultimately, when we truly see God, we see Love itself. Our daily focus, on whatever mountain of culture we influence, must be to discover what God as Love looks like.

God is quite intentional with the ways He shows us His love and therefore asks us to represent His love to others the same way. Love isn't some ethereal concept or a mere feeling. Love actually looks like something. It's an action that has been done intentionally—tangible proof that something or someone is valued and important. When we think about God's love for us, we don't have to guess or wonder what His heart is towards us because He sent Jesus as proof of His love. God is love. He is alive and has always lived with great intention towards us—involved in the details of our lives, even when we don't recognize it in the moment. Whatever your role is on your mountains, find ways to express His love and people's value to Him through the details, the excellence, and the way you serve. Reformers must intentionally ascend the mountains by going up in the opposite spirit of what is presently ruling there. In each chapter about the seven distinct mountains, you will better understand practical ways to do this.

7. A REFORMER MUST UNDERSTAND THE ROLE OF THE CHURCH ON THE SEVEN MOUNTAINS

Jesus said, "I will build My church and the gates of hell
will not prevail against it."
Matthew 16:18

The interesting thing here about the word translated "church" is that Jesus chose the Greek word *Ekklesia*. It was not a religious word, which was in keeping with Jesus' general way of communicating. The words for church of that day were temple (*hieron*) or synagogue (*synagogue*). However, Jesus didn't say, "I will build my temple." nor "I will build my synagogue." He intentionally used a non-religious Greek word that was very well known in the context of civic duty. Ekklesia means "a gathering of citizens called out of their homes into some public place of the council for the purpose of deliberating on public matters." This understanding underscores the seven-mountain assignment of bringing the influence of the kingdom of God into the main public spheres. It is His built up *Ekklesia* in the seven areas of culture that has authority over the gates of hell. It is not from the temple or synagogue or a church building that authority is exerted, but from the public seats of authority where the gates of hell operate.

The seven-mountain template provides a practical framework for understanding that we must take the gospel of the kingdom outside of the four walls of the church. We must shift from *synagogue* thinking into *Ekklesia* thinking. Studies show that most church congregants will never have a traditional full-time ministry call. The majority are called out as the *Ekklesia* to bring heavenly influence into the seven primary public places of society. We can value the buildings we call church with its ministers on the Mountain of Religion, but everything and everyone else must rise outside of that and find a function on the other six council seats of culture.

Statistics tell us that only 3% of church members will ever have a role in traditional ministry. That leaves 97% feeling like second-class citizens in the kingdom of God because they wrongly assume that if God really wanted to use them He would have put them behind a pulpit on the Mountain of Religion. The other mountains provide plenty of platforms and pulpits for ministry, they just look different. The Lord desires that all of the Church be activated in ministry throughout our entire work week. He wants each of us, with our different careers, talents, and passions to feel validated in what we do.

The role of the local church, whatever style and expression, is important because it's where we gather to worship, become equipped and refreshed as reformers, and sent back out into our assignments.

"Now it will come to pass in the last days that the mountain of the Lord's house will be established on the top of the mountains, and will be exalted above the hills, and people will flow to it. Many nations will come and say, 'Come let's go up to the mountain of the Lord... He will teach us His ways and we will walk in His paths.'"
Micah 4:1-2

CHAPTER TWO

HOW TO USE THIS REFERENCE MANUAL

The following seven chapters will provide details for each of the seven mountains. Each chapter will cover 10 main points that reformers need to know about each mountain of culture. Here is a brief description of each section to help you better understand those points:

1. THE ITES, PRINCIPALITIES, AND DEMONIC STRATEGY ON THE MOUNTAINS

In this section of each chapter, we will connect the meaning of the name of each of the "Ites" to the meaning of the name of the principality and his demonic strategy on that mountain. Just as God's people followed the ark of His presence into the Promised Land, so will our generation follow Jesus' ministry on earth in unfamiliar ways into the greatest ending to the greatest story of all. Deuteronomy 28 declared that the Israelites would be the head and not the tail *if* they accepted the mission to go into their land of inheritance. God told us in Psalm 2:8 to "Ask of Me and I will give you the nations for your inheritance." Our promised land is the seven mountains, or foundations of power, and our inheritance is the nations of the world—all of which rightfully belong to God. It was God's idea that we no longer be the tail, but that we be the head and find His strategy and anointing to rid each of the seven sectors of society of the enemy's lies there. As the Lord brings us into this land, like the Israelites, we will encounter seven aspects of the enemy of God that are "greater and mightier" than us (as in Deuteronomy 7:1). Joshua's enemies were the Hittites, the Girgashites, the Amorites, the Canaanites, the Perizzites, the Hivites, and the Jebusites. For us, those "Ites" nations have a meaning that corresponds to the present demonic stronghold on each of the seven mountains that shape society:

Media, Family, Arts & Entertainment, Economy, Religion, Education, and Government.

All seven of the principalities have the same basic mission:

1. Prevent the particular face of God on that mountain from being restored to society.
2. Prevent humanity from experiencing the love of God that was meant to be displayed on that mountain.
3. Prevent people from knowing the primary big truth about God that was meant to be expressed on that mountain.
4. Prevent people from experiencing a healed perspective of the goodness of God through each of the mountains, which were ultimately meant to assure us of certain things about us.

Ultimately there is one enemy, Satan, on each of the mountains—but He uses His demons and principalities to deceive people into believing lies about God, about themselves, and about the best way for that mountain to function. When we believe lies we act on them and then reap the consequences of those lies, further perpetuating the lies through the broken systems of culture we have established. This cycle can be interrupted, but we must first stop fighting each other and recognize the real enemy.

2. THE ARCHANGELS ON THE MOUNTAINS

In this section of each chapter, we will connect the meaning of the name of the mighty archangel to the assignment he has on each of the mountains. Each one serves the Lord of Hosts and the sons and daughters of God with a host of angel armies that operate in the spirit realm to restore the full image of God in the earth on that particular mountain.

Not only do we each individually have guardian angels assigned to us, but we also have help from powerful archangels that God has assigned to each mountain. When you know the authority and responsibility given to you and you are "wearing your uniform" in the spirit as an ambassador of the King, there is an exponential increase of the release of favor and potential that can take place through your life. Angels will be assigned to you to assist you because, as a reformer, you're not just living for yourself or to survive, but you understand that where you live and work is your mission field and platform.

Most Christians don't have a problem with us identifying the demonic principalities by name and so hopefully you won't be offended that we identify those angelic warriors who fight on our side. For some reason we get crazy when we recognize angels and archangels and inevitably someone will say, "We need to be careful not to worship angels"—as if naming angels is synonymous with worshiping them. It's actually important to personalize what our archangels are capable of doing by listing their names. It reminds us that there are truly more for us than against us and no darkness can compare to the light we've been given.

The specific names of the principalities and archangels that are named in each chapter are extra biblical revelation and cannot be proven. This is not meant to be doctrine nor for purposes of presenting any new teaching that violates sound doctrine. The Bible tells us by name about Jezebel, Baal, Apollyon, Mammon, the Prince of Greece, Lucifer, and Beelzebub on the dark side and about Michael and Gabriel on the good side. The idea that there are dark principalities and good archangels is widely accepted and believed. We have added some names and speak of assignments more specifically than we can prove. It is really not important if the detailed names are right or wrong as the main point is we do have this caliber of angels on our side.

The additional names we discuss come from the book of Enoch which is not a book of the Bible, but a book spoken of in the Bible. It was ruled ineligible to be canonized as scripture because it was clearly contaminated by someone splicing their own revelation into aspects of it. However, clearly a core part of it is truth which is where the seven archangels are listed. Each archangel's name ends in EL, which means *God, the Lord*. Each has an assignment to restore an aspect of the face of God to society and comes with millions of accompanying angels of light.

3. THE FACES OF GOD ON THE MOUNTAINS

In this section of each chapter, we will connect each mountain of culture with an aspect of God, or face of God, that is being restored to society. In the same way that each of us is more than just a man or woman, we have many "faces" such as mother or father, daughter or son, doctor or nurse, teacher or police officer, etc. Who we are could potentially be experienced in a variety of ways. In much the same way God is Father, Son, and Holy Spirit—but who He is to us and for us can be experienced countless ways.

In terms of culture, we were meant to experience God in seven distinct ways:

Communicator in Media

Papa in Family

Creator in Arts & Entertainment

Provider in Economy

Redeemer in Religion

Teacher in Education

King in Government

Revelation 4:5 speaks of "seven blazing flames of fire which are the seven Spirits of God." These are the seven faces or aspects of God reformers are called to re-image in the earth in each respective mountain. Revelation 5:6 describes a Lamb having "seven horns and seven eyes, which are the seven Spirits of God sent out into all the earth." These seven Spirits of God are the seven faces of God on the mountains.

The seven Spirits of God are a part of the weaponry we are equipped with for our seven-mountain assignment. It is not just an assignment He has given us but an assignment that He fully equips us for—with who He is. We are to partner with the blazing flames of fire of who God is. His "horns" of power and presence are what ultimately accomplish the dispossessing of the illegally occupying demonic forces. His "seven eyes" provide the insight we need. Jesus, the Lamb that was slain, took the legal scroll with seven seals that the Father was holding, satisfying the blood price of redemption for regaining the legal authority which was lost by Adam and Eve's sin.

The seven faces of God must be restored in culture so that the earth can truly be filled with the knowledge of the glory of God. Said another way, the world is going to know how absolutely wonderful, powerful, and beautiful our God is.

4. THE COLORS OF OUR RAINBOW GOD ON THE MOUNTAINS

In this section of each chapter, we will connect each color of the rainbow with a corresponding mountain of culture. We will briefly explain the logical and spiritual connection, as well as what the color is known for in chromotherapy (the study and science of healing through colors). Revelation 4:3 tells us that there's a full rainbow around the throne of God, which is why we often refer to Him as our Rainbow God. In Genesis 9:13 God said, "I have set *My* rainbow in the clouds, and it will be a sign of the covenant between *Me* and the earth." He doesn't just call it *the* rainbow or *a* rainbow. God intentionally calls it *His* rainbow, which clearly helps us understand that rainbows represent *who He is*.

Not only is God one and three (as in the Trinity), but He's also seven. 1, 3, and 7, as in the seven Spirits of God. The rainbow is the perfect picture of this glorious and mysterious reality. A rainbow is 1 in that it's actually white light that displays to us as 7 colors when sun and rain interact as a prism effect, with 3 of those colors being the primary colors which all other colors come from—and happen to be the colors of fire. Scripture reveals to us that our God is a consuming fire. When you put all of this together you realize that the seven mountains and the seven Spirits of God each carry an attached color of the rainbow as a visible expression of the nuanced different expressions of this one beautiful God when we see and experience Him in His fullness.

As we look at the seven colors and connect them to their respective mountains be aware that it's not just some new-age concept, but actually scientific. All colors have their own unique sound and frequency, created by our Rainbow God.

5. THE WAYS GOD'S LOVE IS DISPLAYED ON THE MOUNTAINS

In this section of each chapter we will connect the seven mountains to seven things the Lamb is worthy to receive from Revelation 5:12.

> *"Worthy is the lamb that was slain to receive POWER*
> *and RICHES and WISDOM and STRENGTH and*
> *HONOR and GLORY and BLESSING."*
> ***Revelation 5:12***

Worthy is the lamb to receive each of these SEVEN ways He has loved us! When we receive and model any of God's seven primary attributes of love we are in essence restoring His correct image, or the truth about who He is, on earth. He receives what we have become and displayed on earth. We are becoming back to God what He has provided for us and through us to others.

Sometimes we refer to this as the Revelation 5:12 template because it's a template of sorts for us to understand, not just that God loves us, but exactly how He loves us. What does love look like on the seven mountains? God doesn't just love us in theory. His love is expressed in a nuanced way that is unique on each mountain. It is love in action and it expresses His genuine care for us through practical solutions in every area of our lives and our culture. On each mountain God's love is experienced in a nuanced way. When God's love is communicated through the unique way it was originally intended in each area of culture, it registers on the heart of the recipient as one of these seven distinct attributes of His nature: power, riches, wisdom, strength, honor, glory, and blessing.

The verse in Revelation is from a time when John was taken to heaven and shown heaven's response to the reality of Jesus being slain as the Lamb, the One found worthy to open the scroll. All of heaven rejoiced and John heard them sing a new song— "Worthy is the lamb...to receive..." These are seven distinct attributes of heaven and of God. This new song is actually a template for the reformation of culture and the restoration of His full face to society. It clarifies our assignment to know God in an expanded and nuanced way and to make Him known. That is how the knowledge of His glory will fill all the earth.

6. THE BIG LIE ABOUT GOD ON EACH OF THE MOUNTAINS

In this section of each chapter, we will connect each mountain to one central lie that is currently being perpetuated about God through the broken systems. When we interact with those systems the enemy wants us to have a very specific takeaway and distorted view of God.

When we speak of the lie that's being perpetuated on each mountain, the word perpetuated means it's happening over and over again in a cyclical way. When a lie is being perpetuated it's because we have believed a lie based on the consequences that we have reaped in our own lives. For instance, if we're believing something false about God, then we're going to reap the consequences of the broken system that we've put into place based on the wrong thinking we have about His lack, involvement, or distance.

7. HOW THE LIES ABOUT GOD ON EACH MOUNTAIN PLAY OUT IN CULTURE

In this section of each chapter, we will explain some of the ways each particular lie about God on each mountain actually plays out in culture.

To reform each area of culture, we have to recognize that culture itself speaks a truth or a lie to every heart, depending on if that mountain is in synchronicity with God's image or not.

Everywhere His image is not seen, the lie about Him will tend towards producing an orphan mentality in us. The collective hearts of cities and nations are no different than our individual hearts. The same God that knows how to heal and restore an individual person's heart, how to go after the specific lies we've individually believed, and bring truth and freedom to those places—also knows how to deal with the collective hearts of cities and nations.

We'll see how the truth about God, viewed through each of His seven faces, reveals His love and overcomes each specific lie that exalts itself against the knowledge of God. The true battle front is always over the knowledge of God—His correct reputation being seen in the earth.

The goal and the promise is that the whole earth will be filled with the knowledge of the glory of God—*who* He is and *how* He is. More than what the enemy is doing, and more than any other measurable outcome—this is the important mission. Our main objective is to see our God's full-spectrum-face shine in society. It's a relational assignment of first seeing Him in an expanded way and then showcasing Him in that same way.

8. THE BIG TRUTH ABOUT GOD ON EACH OF THE MOUNTAINS

In this section of each chapter, we will connect the primary truth about God that we were ultimately meant to experience on each mountain. Each of these truths will displace the big lie that is currently being perpetuated about Him in the corresponding areas of culture.

The devil has no even remote capacity to challenge God and His power. None. Being a deceiver, he has gone through seasons where he has deceived himself into thinking he can, but every time he has paid a severe price for his self-delusion. Once God the Father said the word "Enough!" Michael and his angels dealt with Lucifer and his angels so quickly it made their heads spin. God observes patiently, often for long periods of time, and when He does Satan grows in momentary self-delusion. The truth is God created Lucifer with a word and He can make Him disappear the same way. Were Satan not a key strategic pawn in God's greatest story of all times, he would already be gone. Furthermore, when the devil has finished his usefulness to the majestic storyline our Father is telling, we know that he will be thrown into the lake of fire made specifically for him. In the glory of His story, God has those made in His image (us) to be the executors of Satan's final judgment. Romans 16:20 tells us the God of peace will crush Satan under our feet.

Satan is the father or source of lies and so he finds himself at times falling for his own lies. However, the truth is that Satan is limited to his substantial abilities to lie and deceive. The Bible says we will one day look at him in amazement and shake our heads that one so pitiful could do so much harm through his lies (Isaiah 14:16). His assault from the beginning has been against us truly knowing God. The initial evil in Lucifer's heart was that he didn't want God looking forward to having close companionship with those made in His image. Call it envy. God always wanted to give away more love. Satan always wanted to take more attention and glory. He presented Adam and Eve with an alternative knowledge (a lie) that conspired against who God is. They fell by eating of the tree of this other knowledge. Lucifer was initially pleased because his competition for attention was seemingly eliminated. He had all kinds of surprises awaiting him and he still does.

"For the weapons of our warfare are not carnal but mighty for the pulling down of strongholds. Casting down arguments and every high thing that exalts itself against the knowledge of God."
2 Corinthians 10:4

The front lines in this great battle is over the true "knowledge of God." Who is He? How is He? Why is He? What is He? If His image is not distorted He is irresistible. In every mountain Satan's primary strategy is to use lies to defeat the true nuanced knowledge of God that is supposed to be exhibited in that are of society. Our primary strategy is truth. We must learn to recognize distortions of who God is and cast them down. A demonic principality is empowered by the belief in his lies. We decimate the lies, not by focusing on them, but by revealing the truth of who God is right in the midst of the counterfeit. Satan is not the stronghold—the lie that he's selling is the stronghold. There is no greater need and no higher strategy on each mountain than to identify the mountain-specific lie that Satan is advancing. In 1 Kings 18 Elijah confronts the prophets of Baal and without a long speech about how wrong the people are, he simply displays the supernatural power of the one true God, allowing each person to see the lie they had believed for themselves. As they do they cry out with realization, "The Lord He is God!

The Lord He is God!" Satan and his principalities fall like lightning from heaven whenever we replace his lies with truth. Again, he has no real power of his own—we empower him by our belief in his lies. This is a spiritual battle of competing knowledges.

9. OUR ASSURANCES ON THE MOUNTAINS

In this section of each chapter, we will connect each mountain of culture to a particular assurance. When the specific face of God on each mountain is correctly displayed it assures us individually and collectively of specific things we were meant to be assured of by God. In the same way that when we are raised in a healthy family the goal is to grow up one day having known, not simply that we are loved, but how we are loved. For example, we are convinced we're truly loved when our home life made us feel protected, taken care of financially, listened to, etc. Similarly, our experiences with each area of culture were ideally meant to communicate God's love for us in very specific ways. Remember we have a propensity to connect our circumstances to what we think God's heart is towards us, at least on a subconscious level.

10. HOW TO PARTNER WITH GOD AND FULFILL OUR ASSIGNMENTS AS REFORMERS ON THE MOUNTAINS

In this section of each chapter, we will provide you with a list of some of the ways you can practically fulfill your unique assignment on the mountains you're called to influence.

And finally, in each chapter we've given you a sense of God's heart towards you and His voice from *His* perspective on that mountain. These are meant to help you connect to the relational priority that it all comes back to—you knowing God like He knows you—and out of that overflow your response to the purpose He had in mind when He first dreamed of you. You were placed here into your story, in this generation, at this time in history because God had an intentional plan for you—for you to know Him, to make Him known, to learn how to be loved by Him, and to radically and extravagantly give that love away.

The media's the most powerful
entity on earth.
They have the power to make the
innocent guilty and to make the
guilty innocent, and that's power.
Because they control the minds
of the masses.

— Malcolm X

CHAPTER THREE

THE MOUNTAIN OF MEDIA

Are you ready to expand your perspective about God on the Mountain of Media? We'll begin with a quick overview and then delve into the details.

In the area of culture referred to as MEDIA (how life is reported), we see God as COMMUNICATOR, the color RED. He is LOVE displayed as BLESSING. This is the blessing that comes to our hearts and our nations when love is communicated. Just as words spoken over us as individuals affect our personal identity, words spoken through media outlets also affect the identity of a city or nation. Media can be a tool to receive the blessing of knowing that we fit into a good plan of a good God, even when immediate circumstances tempt us to believe that we are victims of random circumstances apart from the sovereignty of God. Media that blesses presents truth through a hopeful perspective that gives the listener the ability to envision a happy ending, even when it's news that is difficult to hear. Satan uses the principality APOLLYON (DESTROYER) and the demonic strategy of the HITTITES (TERROR and FEAR) to distort the truth of who God is. God has given us a mighty archangel, GABRIEL, to fight for those called to this mountain. The LIE being perpetuated about God in the current MEDIA OUTLETS is: GOD DOESN'T HAVE A GOOD PLAN FOR US. The TRUTH that we will learn to display in MEDIA is: GOD DOES HAVE A GOOD PLAN FOR US.

1. THE HITTITES AND THE PRINCIPALITY APOLLYON: THE DEMONIC STRATEGY ON THE MOUNTAIN OF MEDIA

The word Hittite means *terror* or *fear* and speaks of the enemy's strategy to flood the Mountain of Media with bad news to induce terror and fear.

The HITTITES were one of the seven nations the Israelites had to conquer in order to obey God and take their promised land. They represent the demons of fear that operate on the Mountain of Media, as well as the strategy to influence the modern news media, which focuses overwhelmingly on negative news and headlines.

APOLLYON is Satan's illegal principality on the Mountain of Media. His name means *destroyer* and he promotes fear-based reporting to do just that. The

demonic strategy is to flood the Mountain of Media with a hopeless narrative of bad news in order to induce terror and fear into the hearts of individuals, as well as into the collective hearts of cities and nations. Apollyon destroys trust in God through the news outlets and uses broken people in the broken news and social media platforms to enslave people by magnifying our fears and causing us to feel unsafe as a society.

People who communicate news and work in various news agencies and TV channels are not the enemy. Even the most irresponsible reporters and those in media who are driven by money and ratings are not the problem. They are often participating with Satan and the demonic realm without realizing it. The true enemy is Satan, the father of lies, who doesn't want us to live free from fear because, when we do, his lies are over. He convinces us through our own circumstances and through the steady stream of bad news from mass media sources that there is no plan, only random tragedy and chaos. As we now have access to the tragic news of billions of lives around the world, our hearts are reinforced to believe the lie that if there is a God, He is not in charge. This lie that releases terror and fear destroys people's perspectives of God, their hope, and even their immune systems.

Apollyon's Strategy:

1. Prevent the face of God as Communicator from being restored to society.
2. Prevent humanity from having access to the truth of how God loves us through the ways He communicates by blessing us.
3. Prevent people from knowing that God has a plan for their life and that He's able to sovereignly execute that plan even while we have freedom to make our own choices.
4. Prevent people from experiencing a healed perspective of the goodness of God through the Mountain of Media, which was ultimately meant to assure us that we have a destiny.

2. THE ARCHANGEL GABRIEL FIGHTS ON THE MOUNTAIN OF MEDIA

GABRIEL means "Messenger of God" — His name reveals His assignment which is to assist in restoring the image of God in the earth as Communicator.

There is no greater privilege than to carry or communicate the message of the gospel (good news). Gabriel was given the supreme privilege of sharing the best news earth had ever heard when he announced to Mary that she would birth Jesus, the Son of God. Gabriel and his host of angel armies serve the Lord of Hosts by helping the sons and daughters of God who are called to impact the Mountain of Media. They are focused on our mission to find and communicate truthful news in a unique way through God's hopeful perspective. Ultimately Gabriel fights with us to overcome the demonic realm through good-news reporting that leaves our hearts knowing that God's still in control.

3. THE FACE OF GOD AS COMMUNICATOR ON THE MOUNTAIN OF MEDIA

God loves with His words and with the way He communicates. When we look at who God is as Communicator, we see that everything He's about has to do with good news and good reports presented in the context of uplifting, restorative, redemptive, and relational conversation that's rooted in hope—even when the facts may be difficult to hear. Even when God corrects, He always reveals a way out and a hopeful end. When He requires repentance, He contextualizes it in the promise of a good outcome, either in this life or for eternity.

All communication started within the heart of a God who communicates. It shouldn't surprise us that communication is accelerating on earth because it is sourced from God Himself, who is alive, advancing, and always pursuing authentic intimacy with every human heart. True intimacy requires trust, speaking and listening, hearing and being heard, understanding and being understood. God created us so we could not only be known by Him, but also know Him. We have the opportunity to truly know Him because He is a God who is constantly communicating with us if we have the hunger and ability to recognize how He is speaking to us.

Communication, like all other aspects of who God is, cannot be separated from the essence of who He is—love personified. Love saw the end before time began, and evidently the end makes the ups and downs of history worth it all. There simply must be a very happy ending to what He started. A good God will make sure of it. Can you imagine the Creator who looked at each part of His creation and said, "It is good!" being a God who allows His creation to just fizzle out? Would He leave us, the object of His affection, to think He had a lousy plan? Not this God. Not a God who is good and wants us to know His goodness—a Papa who wants His children to know His heart for them. Ultimately, communication that has any value happens in the context of God's master plan—a plan that definitely has a happy ending that was intentionally designed, from beginning to end, out of His great love for us.

God as Communicator is the aspect of Himself that speaks as one who already knows the happy ending. God as Communicator will always speak the whole truth to us motivated out of love for us. His words, how and what He communicates, are always full of life, hope, possibility, and the perspective that whatever we are going through can be overcome and can end with us growing in our understanding of Him. How do you know when it's God that's communicating with you? You know because God's communication leaves you feeling like there is something greater that you are being prepared for that makes all that you are going through worthwhile.

4. THE COLOR RED ON THE MOUNTAIN OF MEDIA

Red is the color connected to the Mountain of Media because it typically makes us think of stop signs and yield signs, red traffic lights, special alerts, and breaking news—which all signal a need to pay attention because something important is being communicated.

In chromotherapy, the study and science of healing through colors, it has been identified that the color red may benefit the circulatory and nervous system. Bad news can potentially bring fear and stress that affects our nerves and heart by raising blood pressure. Conversely, news that carries hope can be a factor in protecting and healing our nervous and circulatory systems.

5. GOD'S LOVE DISPLAYED AS BLESSING ON THE MOUNTAIN OF MEDIA

"Worthy is the lamb that was slain to receive power
and riches and wisdom and strength and
honor and glory and BLESSING."
Revelation 5:12

Worthy is the lamb to receive blessing! When we receive and model any of God's seven primary attributes of love we are in essence restoring His correct reputation on earth. He receives what we have become and displayed on earth.

NOTES

We are becoming back to God what He has provided for us and through us to others.

God doesn't just love us in theory. His love is expressed in a nuanced way that is unique on each mountain. It is love in action and it expresses His genuine care for us through practical solutions in every area of our lives and our culture. On the Mountain of Media, God's love is experienced as blessing. When love is communicated through media and news it registers on the heart of the recipient as blessing. The dictionary describes a blessing as "a beneficial thing for which one is grateful" and also as "God's favor." When love is expressed and hits its target in our hearts, it's a benefit to us, and we're grateful for it. Our hearts are wired to accept any love as ultimately the favor of God toward us. When we go through hard times and feel unloved or cursed (the opposite of blessed), we tend to believe that God doesn't love, favor, or bless us. Even if we think we have our belief (or lack of belief) in God all neat and tidy in one corner of our heart, the reality is that we all have an innate sense that we are loved or not loved by God based on whether or not we have determined if He has blessed us.

Why does God's blessing mean so much to us? A blessing goes beyond what someone thinks about us and into what they actually say about us or to us. Words are literally a source of life and death to us because it was the voice and words of our Creator that spoke us into reality and even now sustain us. Words, as well as other forms of communication, cause us to feel loved or rejected. A lack of words and other forms of communication can equally contribute to a sense of being rejected and unvalued. Sometimes, what is never said is the most painful of all.

Our word for blessing comes from the Greek word "eulogia," from which we get the word eulogy. It literally means "good word." At a funeral, when we eulogize someone who has died, we share what we thought about that person and what they meant to us. No matter how awful the person may have been, we always find something positive or redemptive to speak about them. We find the silver lining or good news of their life story and try to create some level of a happy ending to it, right? In a similar way, when our communication is sourced from love, what we speak will be the truth presented from a perspective of an eventual happy ending and will therefore bless those who hear it. Even when it's information that is difficult to hear, it will bring life and remembrance of the goodness of God.

News, and therefore media, has the power to bless us by touching our core beliefs about God, even if nothing is directly said about God or religion. The

way in which news is presented can cause our hearts to fear or to trust—fear the future as random victims of circumstance or trust that somehow the difficult things we go through are an important part of a bigger purpose.

6. THE BIG LIE ABOUT GOD ON THE MOUNTAIN OF MEDIA: GOD DOESN'T HAVE A GOOD PLAN FOR US

Every time we're exposed to the Mountain of Media, the enemy wants our takeaway to be, "We're all just victims of random tragedy and crisis. The whole world is falling apart and my world probably is too."

The big lie about God that's currently being perpetuated on the Mountain of Media—that He doesn't have a viable, good plan for our lives, our nations, and humanity itself—is actually a lie within a lie. Even if we're able to somehow hang on to the correct perspective that God does have a good plan for our lives, when we hear a constant stream of bad news, it becomes unbelievable that He's powerful enough to actually accomplish His good plans in the light of how out of control and random everything seems to be in this world filled with evil and suffering.

It's certainly not the media's fault that bad things happen, but in doing their job to make the facts available to the public, even responsible reporting can propagate this lie about God. When information is presented as matter of fact, devoid of a compassionate and heartfelt response and rarely followed up by a hopeful conclusion, then we're left to assume that is God's heart—that He is distant and focused on the facts, untouched by what's happening to us and the world. With reporters unaware of it, they speak and our hearts translate their words as the curse of all curses—my God, if He exists, is all about the facts, and like a good journalist He never gets involved so as not to taint the reality of the mess I've made or am the victim of.

When we're entertained by or constantly fed the hardships of others, we do so apart from the grace needed to get through it. It's not our crisis, therefore we don't have the grace for it. We watch in horror and at least subconsciously connect to it in such a way that it registers on our psyche and body as if we were the ones going through it. We encounter someone else's pain and translate our response as if it were our reality—a reality of tragedy without God's grace to get through it or see what He's doing in the midst of it.

7. HOW THIS LIE ABOUT GOD ON THE MOUNTAIN OF MEDIA PLAYS OUT IN CULTURE

The freedom of speech, expressed through media, has produced a society of people who are free on the outside but enslaved inside. Media reports are meant to defend our access to truth, but real truth sets you free from the inside out.

Whoever controls the media potentially controls the government. We can also say that whoever controls the media controls the collective heart of a city or nation, affecting the individuals' health and state of mind. The effect of bad news is universal—it disheartens and troubles. Many medical studies, as well as the Bible, tell us that good news literally affects our bodies. There's an intrinsic value to it. Good news can strengthen you physically, and good news is refreshing to a weary soul. Conversely, we can gather that bad news will sicken us and demoralize us. Being exposed continually to bad or tragic news will make people and society itself fearful, sick, and weak.

When we believe, individually and collectively, that God doesn't have a good plan for us, we live enslaved to fear. Fear not only affects our health, it's emotionally exhausting. When we fear, we constantly scramble to control everything we can in order to minimize the possibility for more pain. That control usually gets us into relational problems that turn into more pain, causing more fear and control. We are all pretty typical in our responses to this cycle—addictions, excessive entertainment, shame, greed, or basically any diversion from pain or the fear it causes. God is angry about that cycle—not angry with us, but angry because He hates seeing the ones He loves suffer from the lies we have believed about Him and ourselves. Those working in media who get that heart of His will discover His better ways of communicating news and information. Truly responsible reporting is essentially the finger that dares to reach into the spinning fan of fear and interrupt its perpetual cycle.

8. THE BIG TRUTH ABOUT GOD ON THE MOUNTAIN OF MEDIA: GOD HAS A GOOD PLAN FOR US

Despite the onslaught of bad news and tragic stories we must remind ourselves that God is still all-powerful, no matter how chaotic things get, and that He is good even when it temporarily seems like He isn't.

The good news of the Kingdom is the fact that God is in charge. He has solutions for everything. He works all things together for our good, and our good is to know the real Him. His kingdom, Heaven coming to earth, is ultimately our happy ending. God is mysterious, but He is mysteriously good. In the same way, the fact that God is all powerful and has a good plan feels somewhat mysterious to us. But no doubt, His plan is mysteriously good and He is capable of accomplishing it, causing all things to work towards our eventual good.

9. OUR ASSURANCE ON THE MOUNTAIN OF MEDIA: YOU HAVE A DESTINY

When the face of God as Communicator is correctly displayed as Blessing on the Mountain of Media it assures us that we each individually and collectively have a destiny.

God has a good plan for every person's life. No one is just a random victim that He has overlooked. God is intentional with our lives and always has a plan of redemption for everyone's story and all that they've been through. As we have real relationship with Him we can experience the destiny He has for us.

10. PARTNER WITH GOD AS COMMUNICATOR ON THE MOUNTAIN OF MEDIA

In order to properly fulfill our assignment on the Mountain of Media we must truly know God as Communicator ourselves, learn to reflect who He is as Communicator personally, and then connect it to the way we observe and report the news. We must become experts on this aspect of God's love and then give it away to all who are influenced by our role on this mountain.

A REFORMER'S ASSIGNMENT ON THE MOUNTAIN OF MEDIA:

1. Carry a heart of good news and a hopeful perspective in your own life so that you can bring it into your professional role in an authentic way. What you contend for personally will easily overflow from you in the workplace. Ask God to reveal His true heart towards you: "For I know the thoughts that

I think toward you, says the Lord, thoughts of peace and not of evil, to give you a future and a hope." Jeremiah 29:11

2.   Accurately find and report the most redemptive angle possible on bad news. Infuse every stage of getting a story or information out to the public with a hopeful perspective that helps the listener or viewer recognize the potential for a happy ending. It's always there, but you must be willing to work harder to find it.

3.   Don't feel a need to blatantly promote religion, God, or salvation through Christ in order to have a positive impact. Any news that promotes peace registers as the good news to a person's heart that God reigns in the earth—at least on a subconscious level.

4.   The goal is not to have Christians reporting bad news, which still facilitates Apollyon's goal of destroying us through terror and fear. The goal is to change the media system itself and fill the world with good news that neutralizes bad news.

5.   Use Philippians 4:8 as a standard for responsible news reporting: "Whatever things are true, noble, just, pure, lovely, and of a good report, if there is any virtue or anything praiseworthy, think on (report) these things." Infuse the world with good news that neutralizes the effects of bad news.

6.   Understand that people are given grace by God to handle our personal problems and setbacks, but not the collective suffering of billions of people on the planet.

7.   Uphold the conviction that life and death are in the power of the tongue by intentionally and strategically communicating life.

8.   Do not allow the enemy to use your reporting to minimize God in the eyes of those watching by only presenting the problem without the solution. Even when you must report something negative, make sure to present it in the context of the truth of the bigger picture and potential for a happy ending or justice to be seen.

NOTES

9. Be willing to find and report the story behind the obvious story. This reassures the collective heart of society, as well as our own hearts that there is a God who is working on our behalf behind the scenes. Use your influence in media to draw attention to the works of redemption that God is doing on the earth right in the midst of heartache and suffering.

10. Don't be deceived into thinking your role as a Christian is to constantly warn others of what could possibly go wrong and pass along information that provokes fear and accomplishes nothing truly helpful.

11. Consider the implications of your choices on the overall psyche of society. Understand that it is irresponsible reporting to replay something horrific and tragic over and over again just because it will increase ratings. It is irresponsible journalism to write and talk incessantly about things that might happen to a minuscule percentage of the population, just because our fear of the unknown provokes us to stop and listen.

12. Always report the news objectively. The obvious news is not necessarily the news. In fact, it's rarely the important thing taking place on the planet. Just because it can make us stop and stare, doesn't mean it's worth reporting. Just because something is a fact, doesn't mean it reflects the overall truth. Facts are based on the micro, or obvious things. Truth is based on the macro, or the bigger picture that's harder to see and report. Facts present a subjective reality. Truth presents an objective reality.

Whenever we use our media outlets to provide others with evidence that God is in charge and He is ever-present, then it makes the truth believable—that God not only has a good plan for our lives and our nations, but despite the presence of evil, He is able to execute His plans.

FOR MORE IN-DEPTH INFORMATION ON THESE TOPICS IN OUR OTHER RESOURCES:

The Seven Mountain Prophecy (Ch 5, Overview)

The Seven Mountain Mantle (Ch 14)

The Seven Mountain Mandate Video Course and Workbook (Session 5)

Rainbow God: The Seven Colors of Love (Ch 6)

Rainbow God Video Course and Workbook (Session 2)

The Seven Mountain Renaissance (Ch 10)

GOD AS COMMUNICATOR

My sons and daughters, don't you know that I hold you and all things together? Not one move is made that I haven't seen, that I haven't planned for, and set a course into motion towards redemption. You look at the obvious, but I'm always working, changing, shifting from behind. Just because you cannot see Me at work, doesn't mean I'm not working it all out to your benefit—all is being leveraged for your good.

I'm the story behind your story—the undercurrent pulling it all back towards Me, towards My heart for you, and towards My better plan. Like invisible guardrails on your destiny, I'm holding it all on the pathway that leads to My goodness. Sure, you see the wind and waves, but can you see where they're taking you, leading you into the depths of My love for you? Nothing is random because I'm not random. My love and My words, My very thoughts towards you, secure you in all your ways.

Although tragedy and crisis come and go, I never leave. I'm the one steady thing that you can depend on. Even when you watch as others are tossed about, you must know that I am with them too. I'm there offering every opportunity for a way out or a grace to overcome. You must remember that I've given each of you grace to overcome anything you go through, but only grace for what you're actually going through. When you don't feel My grace, make sure you haven't entered into someone else's battle. Yes, bear the burdens of others, but don't allow the enemy to entice you into a battle zone I haven't sent you into. Learn to trust that, even if you cannot see Me in their battle, I'm right there with them. Just because you don't see Me watching each and every sparrow, doesn't mean that I don't. It's impossible for Me to look away or walk away from any of My sons and daughters. It makes no difference to Me whether they know they're Mine yet or not. I'm their Father and not only can I not look away, I cannot distance Myself from their every breath—from your every breath.

Every single one that has ever lived or will ever live, has My full attention, has access to My heart towards them, and My unwavering ability to draw them to Myself, to My better ways, to My plans of a future and a hope for them. You have My full attention. You have access to My heart towards you, to My unwavering ability to draw you constantly to Myself and to My better ways. Your life isn't just a series of facts being played out like a sequence of events arranged by chance or the heavy hand of evil. I'm not the news reporter, distant and removed, replaying the choices you've made and the hits you've taken as if I am an outsider looking in. No way! I'm all in it—in every moment and behind every circumstance. I'm not the circumstance, but I'm in it and I'm ready to show you the best way through. But even better, I'm the one ready to make every move with you. Your mess is My mess. Your chaos is My chaos. Your battle is My battle.

I'm speaking, if you'll hear Me—ever communicating, because that's who I am. I'm the voice of love and My love reaches until it finds you—the object of My affection. I'm the whisper from within you that's hard to believe sometimes because it seems too good to be true. I'm the One who's always ready to talk and ready to listen. I'm the consistent voice of blessing over you, that you may be a voice that consistently blesses others. If you listen, you'll hear the steady stream of blessing and passion I have for you, for your world, and for all who live in it with you. Allow Me to teach you to bless like I bless, to see like I see with hope-filled eyes. Be confident in My involvement, in My care, and in My ability to work all things together for good.

What can you do
to promote world peace?
Go home
and love your family.

—Mother Teresa

CHAPTER FOUR

THE MOUNTAIN OF FAMILY

Are you ready to expand your perspective about God on the Mountain of Family? We'll begin with a quick overview and then delve into the details.

In the area of culture referred to as FAMILY, we see God as PAPA, the color ORANGE. He is LOVE displayed as STRENGTH. This is the strength that family was meant to be for us—the strength of bloodline, heritage, and inheritance. It is a generational strength that was meant to help us as individuals stand against the storms of life when everything else falls apart and the one safe place you can always come back to for acceptance and love. Strength, through families, is the foundational fabric of every nation. Satan uses the principality BAAL (PERVERSION) and the demonic strategy of the JEBUSITES (REJECTION) to distort the truth of who God is. God has given us a mighty archangel, RAPHAEL, to fight for those called to this mountain. The LIE being perpetuated about God in the current FAMILY INSTITUTION is: WE HAVE BEEN ABANDONED AND REJECTED BY GOD. The TRUTH about God that we will learn to display in FAMILY is: GOD HAS NOT ABANDONED OR REJECTED US.

1. THE JEBUSITES AND THE PRINCIPALITY BAAL: THE DEMONIC STRATEGY ON THE MOUNTAIN OF FAMILY

The word Jebusite means *a place trodden down* and speaks of the enemy's strategy of using *rejection* on the Mountain of Family.

The JEBUSITES were one of the seven nations the Israelites had to conquer in order to obey God and take their promised land. They represent the demons of rejection that operate on the Mountain of Family, as well as the strategy to create broken families that produce individuals who then have aberrant behavior.

BAAL is Satan's illegal principality on the Mountain of Family and represents *perversion*. His name means *lord*. The demonic strategy is to use rejection to bring individuals and families under his lordship, eroding families and society itself. Baal undermines trust in God through his assault on families, causing generation after generation of broken and hurt people to continue the cycle of hurting others. The result is numerous social and physical ills that spring out of rejection—including depression, fear, sexual deviance, addictions, anger, and violence that cause the eventual breakdown of not only families, but entire communities.

In the Old Testament, the worship of Baal involved ritual homosexual activity, cutting oneself, temple prostitution, and child sacrifice to Molech. He was the fertility god and also masqueraded as important for provision and protection, but in reality was the god of perversion. Sexual identity confusion, self-mutilation, abortions, and infanticide are all evidences of the work of Baal. Our typical way of combatting the moral erosion of society is to attempt to manage external behavior by overcommunicating standards and rules and trying to change laws. Ultimately, we won't prevent or stop abortion, sexual perversion, or the self-harming many do—from the outside-in. Internal matters of the heart will never be healed by external pressures, laws, or ordinances. The Mountain of Family includes anything related to healthcare, medicine, counseling, and healing of any kind. If the breakdown and wound began with rejection in the context of the family dynamic, then it takes nothing less than the heart of God as Papa to heal the wound of rejection with His unconditional love and acceptance, restoring strength to families and communities.

People who are a part of the breakdown of families, no matter how immoral they may be, are not the enemy. Even those who are seeking to establish their own definition of family, or fighting to maintain their rights to abortion, etc are not the problem. Because of their own brokenness and deception, they are often partnering with Satan and the demonic realm without realizing it. The true enemy is Satan, the father of lies, who doesn't want us to live free from rejection, because when we do, his lies are over. He convinces Christians that we must be the rules keepers rather than those known for love and acceptance that properly display the heart of the Father.

Baal's Strategy:

1. Prevent the face of God as Papa from being restored to society.
2. Prevent humanity from having access to the truth of how God loves us as a Father by the way He brings strength to families.
3. Prevent people from knowing that God has never abandoned or rejected us and has unconditional love for us.
4. Prevent people from experiencing a healed perspective of the goodness of God through the Mountain of Family, which was ultimately meant to assure us that we are accepted.

2. THE ARCHANGEL RAPHAEL FIGHTS ON THE MOUNTAIN OF FAMILY

RAPHAEL means "God heals, God please heal, or wholeness is in EL (God)" — His name reveals His assignment which is to assist in restoring the image of God in the earth as Papa.

Family is the foundational fabric of every nation. Without family, there is no fabric of society. To the degree families are fractured and frayed, society is fractured and frayed. In general, strong families engender healthy individuals and fractured families produce sick individuals. Studies show that upwards of 90% of all illnesses are psychosomatic in nature—meaning they have an emotional quotient as their root cause. A damaged emotional state is generally there because of a family dynamic of hurt, abuse, strife or rejection—or an abusive, absent, or deficient father-figure. When our natural father has so failed us, it's hard for there to be a proper perspective of Papa God. Everything and everyone who works towards healing and health is an asset for the institution of family. Raphael and his host of angel armies serve the Lord of Hosts by helping the sons and daughters of God who are called to heal and restore strength to the Mountain of Family. They are focused on our mission to heal the rejection that is at the root of family and societal breakdown. Ultimately Raphael fights alongside us to overcome the demonic realm through the truth of God's unconditional love and acceptance.

3. THE FACE OF GOD AS PAPA ON THE MOUNTAIN OF FAMILY

When we look into the face of God as Papa we see another strand of the love of God. Satan always comes to kill, steal, and destroy families by distorting our perspective of God through negative experiences with our earthly parents, especially our fathers. Our Heavenly Father always comes to heal, protect, and deliver. When we encounter Him as Papa we experience His heart of acceptance, which gives us the sense of belonging we were all meant to have. When we choose to acknowledge Him as our Father, we are adopted into the family of God.

Jesus perfectly revealed the heart of the Father to us in the story of the Prodigal Son (Luke 15). When the son left home to live out his rebellion, squandering all his inheritance and ending up in a literal pigpen, not only was his father ready to forgive his son's choices, but the father instantly put his robe and ring on him, fully restoring the son's identity, authority, and destiny. As soon as he saw his son coming down the road towards him, the father ran to meet his son. Like the father in the story, God is a Father who waits and looks hopefully our way even when we are still in the pigpen of our choices and behavior. The moment we turn His way He's running towards us with open arms and a heart of joy.

Jesus also revealed the heart of God as Papa by the way He responded to the woman caught in adultery who was brought to Him by the most religious ones of that time. They wanted His stance on her sin, but He refused to be pressured into judging her because He knew that His stance on her heart was more important as she was being publicly shamed. After her accusers left Jesus didn't even give her a lecture about how wrong she was, but He made sure she knew that He didn't condemn her. He demonstrated the unconditional love of our Father by not rejecting her and by empowering her saying, "Go and sin no more."

To succeed with our assignment on the Mountain of Family it's not enough to try to police people's external behavior. We're going to have to know the heart of God as Papa so well that we overflow with His unconditional love and acceptance that changes people from the inside-out. Rules inform or condemn. An encounter with God's love goes deep and heals.

4. THE COLOR ORANGE ON THE MOUNTAIN OF FAMILY

Orange is the color connected to the Mountain of Family. It's a mixture of red and yellow—red speaks of our family bloodline and yellow speaks of our individual unique glory. Combining them both, orange represents that part of our Papa's heart that affirms we belong to Him. We are His bloodline. Whatever else you may or may not discover about who you are, you can always know that you are His and you belong in the family of God. It also represents the fact that He not only made each of us to be unique, but He also enjoys what makes you who you are. We each have our own glory or distinct beauty that delights and makes proud the heart of this Father.

In chromotherapy, the study and science of healing through colors, it has been identified that the color orange may assist in the elimination of localized fats and improving energy. Studies suggest that an unhealthy home-life contributes to obesity. When we don't experience the strength of a healthy family that we were meant to, we become weak people living in a weakened society. Strength to resist disease is broken down when family is broken down.

5. GOD'S LOVE DISPLAYED AS STRENGTH ON THE MOUNTAIN OF FAMILY

"Worthy is the lamb that was slain to receive power
and riches and wisdom and STRENGTH and
honor and glory and blessing."
Revelation 5:12

Worthy is the lamb to receive strength! When we receive and model any of God's seven primary attributes of love we are, in essence, restoring His correct reputation on earth. He receives what we have become and displayed on earth. We are becoming back to God what He has provided for us and through us to others.

God doesn't just love us in theory. His love is expressed in a nuanced way that is unique on each mountain. It is love in action and it expresses His genuine care for us through practical solutions in every area of our lives and our culture. On the Mountain of Family God's love is experienced as strength. When love is experienced through a healthy family it registers on the heart of the recipient as strength. The Greek word for strength is *Ischys* which means "used of those joined by the bonds of natural blood." It speaks of a resolve of spirit that is present because of the bonds of family.

Not only does God care for our families, but the idea of families originated in Him. God is love, so what does God as love look like in families? In a family, love looks like strength—strength that stands against the storms of life when everything else falls apart. It's the one thing you can always come back to. A man or woman founded on a healthy family is a strong individual. Of course, strength can still be found in a spiritual family and in friends when there is a breakdown of a person's natural family, but God's first preference is that our natural families provide us with a stable, loving, and secure environment to grow in.

He alone is the perfect Papa and He loves each and every one of us exceedingly above and beyond what we could imagine. This love, and wherever it finds its expression, is our strength. If you have experienced true love of any sort through any source, it came from Him and Him alone. God doesn't just love us. He IS love. And when you find this love, you find your strength. You and I were created to know Him—to know love and to be loved. We were never meant to breathe one breath in this realm apart from knowing, in every cell of our being and in every corner of our heart, that we are loved with a perfect love, unconditionally.

When the strength of family is weakened, the purposes God created family for are lost: protection, procreation, provision, instruction, and identity. When these become eroded, our families are weak, we are weak, and our nations are weak. When we experience each of these purposes for family in a healthy way, we have the opportunity to experience the love of God. When we don't, doors are left open for lies to come creeping in about our Papa's heart toward us.

When we aren't protected by our family, we believe we aren't safe. When we aren't properly provided for and protected, we believe we aren't worth caring for and being protected. When we are left to figure life out for ourselves, we believe we must be a burden and are too complicated to deal with. When our true identity is not spoken into our hearts, we believe we have none. All these lies draw us to one conclusion: we have been abandoned and rejected by God. But His love is stronger than lies.

6. THE BIG LIE ABOUT GOD ON THE MOUNTAIN OF FAMILY: WE HAVE BEEN ABANDONED AND REJECTED BY GOD

Because we were each born into some version of a family we've all been impacted by the Mountain of Family where the enemy wants our takeaway to be, "I'm not truly loved for who I am, I don't really belong, and I'm the only one who really looks out for me."

The big lie about God that's currently being perpetuated about God on the Mountain of Family—that we have been abandoned and rejected by God—is the basic lie that Satan believed himself. He chose to perceive it as rejection when God wanted sons and daughters made in His image. Once he agreed with this lie of rejection his DNA changed from something beautiful to something progressively degenerative and his name was changed from Lucifer (light bearing) to Satan (accuser).

Perceived rejection can cause as much damage as actual rejection. Unfortunately, even believers are susceptible to this lie, and it at times can be compounded in the house of God, where distorted teachings can tell us that being imperfect has us deserving rejection and abandonment. Once we agree with this BIG LIE it opens us up to the lordship of Baal and all sorts of identity challenges. It becomes imperative for those called to this mountain that they understand this is the front lines of battle and exceeds in importance the contending for laws that encourage better behavior or morality.

NOTES

Good laws are good laws, but they don't change hearts as they are an outside-in dynamic. Only encountering the unconditional love and acceptance of God affects the heart and makes a change go inside-out. The kingdom of God is always an inside-out dynamic. Good laws are good for order but only encountering the Father's love brings freedom. Where the Spirit of the Lord is there is freedom (2 Cor. 3:17)

Satan slanders God in society through broken families and their subsequent fallout. The tool of rejection is the devil's simple lie with which he devastates individuals, families, and ultimately even whole nations.

It's not the whispering of rejection that causes the damage. It's the believing of that lie that causes the damage. This is where Baal and his demons of rejection offer the counterfeit anti-family.

Ultimately rebellion is the choice to join an anti-family "family." Rejection is the wound that opens the door to every sexual perversion. Generally speaking, once someone agrees with the poison of rejection, they will progressively advance with that rejection.

At some point the rejection can even advance to a rejection of one's own sexuality and identity. This is why sexual deviancy cannot be changed by external pressures or laws. Laws can inform on the collective desired norm for society, but it takes grace and unconditional love for the norm to be accessed internally. Healing comes from a fresh revelation of Papa's unconditional love.

7. HOW THIS LIE ABOUT GOD ON THE MOUNTAIN OF FAMILY PLAYS OUT IN CULTURE

The present reality of most families perpetuates the lie and the deep core belief that God has abandoned and rejected us. Rejection, like all good lies, just needs one small entrance and can settle in as a never-ending cycle, generation after generation. If we don't recognize the lie for what it is, then our hurt causes us to hurt others. When we feel rejected, the reason it hurts like no other pain on earth is because of what it subconsciously and ultimately communicates to our heart, that God doesn't love us.

No human can live a quality life under the core belief that the One who created them doesn't truly care for them. The pain of rejection plays out in further rejection of others. To some degree, we all suffer from a level of rejection and therefore tend to judge and reject ourselves and each other. Families become a haven for this lie and we grow up not only feeling rejected but learning to reject others as some sort of dysfunctional survival mechanism. Kids feel rejected by parents, then grow up to cause their kids to feel rejected. Families and individuals transfer that culture of rejection to the larger stage of people groups, religions, races, and economic statuses. Rejection in the home and personal level breeds rejection in every layer of society.

In order to reject, we must first judge if something or someone should be rejected. We've all done it without even thinking about it. Jesus, who knew the heart of our Father better than any of us, spoke constantly about love, but never did He encourage us to size someone up based on their behavior and treat them in a way that would cause them to feel unloved, judged, or rejected. Many Christians say, "Love the sinner, hate the sin." What if we were to love the sinner (starting with ourselves) and that's it? When we consider our right to love others as children of God as greater than our right to protect and uphold our moral values, then this lie that God has rejected us will actually begin to unravel.

8. THE BIG TRUTH ABOUT GOD ON THE MOUNTAIN OF FAMILY: GOD HAS NOT ABANDONED OR REJECTED US

God as Papa is the only One who can heal the core wound of rejection because that wound was ultimately caused by the core belief that God has rejected and abandoned us. No matter how or through whom the enemy was able to make us feel rejection, our hearts all eventually, at least on a subconscious level, were made to feel like the One who has all power should have made sure we grew up being loved and fully accepted. Even those of us who believe that God is love and that He loves us still struggle with the message that is opposite, based on the way we perceive our circumstances and life experiences. Not only has God not abandoned or rejected any of us, He is our perfect Father and He's able to heal both our real and perceived rejection, and show us how to break its devastating cycle in our culture.

9. OUR ASSURANCE ON THE MOUNTAIN OF FAMILY: YOU ARE ACCEPTED

When the face of God as Papa is correctly displayed as Strength on the Mountain of Family it assures us that we all belong, we are all accepted, and we are all loved unconditionally.

God has never abandoned or rejected anyone. He isn't just somewhere far away waiting for us to figure everything out by ourselves. God will always love every person as our perfect Father unless we choose to reject Him. He has never and will never abandon or leave any of His children alone.

10. PARTNER WITH GOD AS PAPA ON THE MOUNTAIN OF FAMILY

In order to properly fulfill our assignment on the Mountain of Family we must truly know God as Papa ourselves, learn to reflect who He is as Papa personally, and then connect it to the way we interact with others, especially with our families. We must become experts on this aspect of God's love and then give it away to all who are influenced by our role on this mountain. Most disease, crime, mental illness, and aberrant lifestyles are a direct result of toxic families—families who have lost their strength. Anyone called to impact the structure of family in any nation's culture is ultimately called to be an agent of healing at every possible level of society. In order to do this, you must personally become an expert on who God is as Papa.

A REFORMER'S ASSIGNMENT ON THE MOUNTAIN OF FAMILY:

1. Carry a heart of a son/daughter that knows how loved and accepted you truly are by Papa so that you can authentically love and accept others in your personal life, as well as in your workplace. "Because you are His sons and daughters, God sent the Spirit of His Son into our hearts, the Spirit who calls out, 'Abba, Father.' So you are no longer a slave, but God's child and since you are His child, God has made you also an heir." Galatians 4:6-7

2. Pursue healing of your own rejection so that you can be an effective carrier of healing to others. As your relationship with God as Papa is restored, you can experience profound fulfillment by participating with His heart to heal families.

3. Don't feel a need to blatantly promote religion, God, or salvation through Christ in order to have a positive impact through your professional or personal role on the Mountain of Family. Any ways that we help someone to feel unconditionally loved and accepted, registers to a person's heart that

God unconditionally loves and accepts them—at least on a subconscious level. When they feel His love, they are more likely to want a relationship with Him, which gives opportunity for freedom from behaviors and the sin that enslaves them.

4. The goal of Christians who influence the Mountain of Family isn't to simply uphold the standard of behavior and continue to be primarily known for what Christians are against. The assignment is to display the acceptance God has for every single person just the way they are in such a way that we then earn the right to offer solutions and healing for areas of pain and deception.

5. Don't try to do what only the Holy Spirit can do in someone's heart—bring conviction of sin. Through us, Papa God can hug the poison of rejection out of even the most dysfunctional souls, but that requires allowing God to love them through us before we ever try to point out their brokenness. Telling people right and wrong has always been easier than loving them through the ugly, messy stages of sin.

6. Don't be afraid of looking like you are condoning someone's sin simply because you are being their friend. Jesus was considered a Friend of Sinners and wasn't afraid of what religious people thought when He spent time with broken, wounded, and deceived people. Obviously, He wouldn't have been considered their friend if all He did was constantly remind them of the standard they were falling short of. Fear casts out love and where love is, fear isn't present. Love and accept others in such a way that they never fear rejection by you or the God you know.

7. Uphold the conviction that God cares more about people than He does about their sin. It is because He cares about us that He cares about the things that come between us and Him (sin).

8. Fight for people's hearts to be healed of their rejection by assuring their love and acceptance more than you fight for external laws. Jesus, God in the flesh and the One who wrote the Ten Commandments, modeled this for us.

The devil is the great rejector. God is the great acceptor. This is the source of our strength—that our original Father is relentlessly for us and no matter our level of failure, no matter the depth of our sin, He still offers Himself to us as Papa.

The assignment on the Mountain of Family is to demolish the lie of rejection that's often perpetuated by the church through presenting conditional love. We must lead with unconditional love. Once we chase off the accusation and lead with unconditional love, perhaps we will have earned the right to empower others as Jesus did to "Go and sin no more."

FOR MORE IN-DEPTH INFORMATION ON THESE TOPICS IN OUR OTHER RESOURCES:

The Seven Mountain Prophecy (Ch 11, Overview)

The Seven Mountain Mantle (Ch 16)

The Seven Mountain Mandate Video Course and Workbook (Session 6)

Rainbow God: The Seven Colors of Love (Ch 3)

Rainbow God Video Course and Workbook (Session 3)

The Seven Mountain Renaissance (Ch 7)

GOD AS PAPA

My sons and daughters, can you see My arms open wide and my heart that has a place in it that literally no one else can satisfy? I'm so proud to be the One who thought of you before time began—the One who waited with joyful expectation for you to come alive to the reality of who I am. I'm your Papa, your Father in heaven. You really do have a Father and I really do exist and I really am for you! I don't have to choose to love you. I cannot help but love you because you're Mine. You came from Me, and if you choose Me, you'll land in My arms, back in My heart, and in your rightful place as My child—with Me forever. I'm a kind of Papa that you've never seen before. You may have had glimpses, but let Me assure you that your greatest desires and expectations pale in comparison. I'm incapable of disappointing you—when it's all seen in the light of eternity. I'm your protector, your strength, the One you can always run to.

Though everything around you and everything you've been through tempts you to believe less than the truth, the truth is, I am your faithful Father. I'm moved by what moves you, by your fears, your pain, your disappointments—but I'm not worried about you. I know what you've been through, the challenges...and I know what I put in you, and what you need to become all that I dreamed for you. I knew your weaknesses and frailties way before you discovered them. I knew the choices you'd make, good and not so good, way before you made them. None of it overwhelms Me or makes me look away or change My mind about you. I've never, nor will I ever give up on you.

I'm not some task master who needs you to perform so that you can fulfill some agenda I've created. I don't need you to behave. In fact, the only reason I care about sin, about what comes between us, is because I care about you. All I've ever wanted from you is a relationship. A real relationship. Intimacy that we both feel. Trust that is mutual and love that's given and received. I can't wait for another day, every day and all of eternity, to be faithful to you and to allow you to live in My unconditional love for you. It's my delight to give you all that is Mine and all that is in Me. You are My sons and My daughters, which means you don't ever have to earn My love and My acceptance. I love you just like you are right now and nothing you could do would make Me love you more or less. I made you to need the strength of family. I made you to need Me, to need us. You have brothers and sisters from the ages, who love you, can't wait to see you, and are cheering for you at this very moment. We are your family and I am your Papa—your strength. I am strong in you and for you. Trust Me and allow me to be your strength so that you can be strong for those who haven't yet discovered they're no longer orphans.

Like the father in the story of the prodigal son, let's wait together at the end of the road. Let's plan their homecoming party together and celebrate their journey home— their journey back into My Papa's heart.

Creativity is
intelligence having fun.

— Albert Einstein

CHAPTER FIVE

THE MOUNTAIN OF ARTS & ENTERTAINMENT

In the area of culture referred to as ARTS & ENTERTAINMENT, we see God as CREATOR, the color YELLOW. He is LOVE displayed as GLORY. This is the glory of God's creativity coming through humanity—through His children who are made in the image of their Creator. When we see the glory of God's creativity coming through others, it was meant to remind us that He loves us enough to give us a glory of our own. Your glory is your uniqueness, what you are known for, and what makes you, you. When you've found the best version of yourself—the you that God created you to be—you've found your true glory. When your true glory causes others to be inspired and entertained, you're expressing an aspect of God as Creator. Satan uses the principality JEZEBEL (SEDUCTION) and the demonic strategy of the HIVITES (COMPROMISE) to distort the truth of who God is. God has given us a mighty archangel, JEHUDIEL, to fight for those called to this mountain. The LIE being perpetuated about God in what the current ARTS & ENTERTAINMENT INDUSTRY promotes is: GOD DOESN'T WANT US TO HAVE FUN. The TRUTH that we will learn to display in ARTS & ENTERTAINMENT is: GOD WANTS US TO ENJOY LIFE.

1. THE HIVITES AND THE PRINCIPALITY JEZEBEL: THE DEMONIC STRATEGY ON THE MOUNTAIN OF ARTS & ENTERTAINMENT

The word Hivite means *village of tents* and by extension speaks of the enemy's strategy to spread across society *compromise* and *defilement* through the Mountain of Arts & Entertainment.

The HIVITES were descendants of Ham and one of the seven nations the Israelites had to conquer in order to obey God and take their promised land. They represent the demons of compromise that operate on the Mountain of Arts & Entertainment, as well as the strategy to desensitize the hearts and minds of society by entertaining us with seemingly harmless things that actually bring death and destruction.

NOTES

JEZEBEL is Satan's illegal principality on the Mountain of Arts & Entertainment and represents *seduction*. Her name means *unchaste* or *Baal is husband*. This principality clearly has a strong association with Baal. The demonic strategy is to seduce people on the Mountain of Arts &Entertainment into all kinds of compromise to distort what real, life-giving creativity and entertainment is. Jezebel seduces, uses, and then destroys those she puts in the spotlight. Bacchus, the god of drunkenness, partners with Jezebel in positioning those on this mountain to compromise, thus becoming essentially pawns for Jezebel's plan to desensitize the soul of society to moral compromise.

People who work on this mountain are not the enemy. Even the most compromising among them who frivolously and irresponsibly use their talent are not the problem. They are often partnering with Satan and the demonic realm without realizing it. The true enemy in this great spiritual war that's taking place over arts and entertainment, and specifically over Hollywood, is Satan. More than anyone, he understands the amazing glory and grandeur of true creativity and knows God's love for creating. Satan loves to poison this area of culture by deceiving the sons and daughters of God. He will use them to either spew his filth through entertainment or cause them to run and hide from it altogether, leaving this entire area of culture void of the real light and life-giving creativity it so desperately needs.

Jezebel will be crushed on the very mountain she has cast these sons and daughters from, but not simply by fasting and prayer meetings of the righteous or by hiding from the overall industry. Jezebel will be crushed by the coming tsunami of God's children who will see and know Him in His creative goodness and light and then re-image Him in all of society. This army of rising sons and daughters will so connect to the Creator that there will be no room left for Jezebel or any desire for her lesser offers. It will become apparent to all that the best music, stories, directing, and creativity of every sort is coming from those who have authentic relationships with God. She will lose her power to entice and addict the ones filled with God's talent and gifts. We are fast forwarding towards that day.

Jezebel's Strategy:

1. Prevent the face of God as Creator from being restored to society.
2. Prevent humanity from having access to the truth of how God displays His love for us in His creation and through the glory of His creativity coming through us as His children.

3. Prevent people from knowing that God wants us to have fun and that He loves it when we enjoy life.

4. Prevent people from experiencing a healed perspective of the goodness of God through the Mountain of Arts & Entertainment, which was ultimately meant to assure us that God enjoys us.

2. THE ARCHANGEL JEHUDIEL FIGHTS ON THE MOUNTAIN OF ARTS & ENTERTAINMENT

JEHUDIEL means "God is glorified, or the glory goes to God" — His name reveals His assignment which is to assist in restoring the image of God in the earth as Creator.

Jehudiel and his host of angel armies serve the Lord of Hosts by helping those who are called to impact the Mountain of Arts & Entertainment. They are focused on the very mission that's hidden in the name Jehudiel—to give all glory back to God, the source of all true creativity. Ultimately, Jehudiel fights with us to display the truth about God as Creator through His sons and daughters who know He wants us to celebrate, have fun, and enjoy life.

3. THE FACE OF GOD AS CREATOR ON THE MOUNTAIN OF ARTS & ENTERTAINMENT

God was first introduced to us as Creator in Genesis chapter one and He has never ceased being the Creator. In fact, creation itself shows us that He's a compulsive creative! If we can't see Him in this way we're going to have a hard time bringing successful reformation to the Mountain of Arts & Entertainment. Many think our primary mission on this mountain is to bring values and the message of salvation to the big screen, but it really isn't. Those are assignments for those on the Mountain of Religion where we showcase the Redeemer face of God. God is joyfully creative, and the manifestation of His creativity brings heaven's wow factor with it to earth. His creativity always reveals His glory and it's meant to deeply touch our emotions.

Psalm 16:11 tells us, "In His presence is FULLNESS of joy, and at His right hand are pleasures forevermore." If God as Creator has the capacity to impact even His throne room of glory with maximum joy and maximum pleasure, then imagine what could happen here on earth as we allow His creativity to flow through us. The creative aspect of God is perhaps the most overlooked and under appreciated by Christians and is a primary reason that we've been less than successful with revealing a God that's delightful to society. God truly is the desire of the nations when He's properly represented as Creator.

4. THE COLOR YELLOW ON THE MOUNTAIN OF ARTS & ENTERTAINMENT

Yellow is the color connected to the Mountain of Arts & Entertainment because it is typically used to highlight and spotlight something or someone. It reminds us of the sun and "having our day in the sun." Isaiah 60 tells us the glory of God is to be seen on us as an antidote to darkness. He wants His creative kids carrying His light and glory into this area of culture.

In chromotherapy, the study and science of healing through colors, it has been identified that the color yellow may be good for improving skin health. Our "skin" is our outward identity. We have a healthier understanding of our identity, who we really are, when we properly showcase God's creativity by allowing Him to shine on and through our talents.

5. GOD'S LOVE DISPLAYED AS GLORY ON THE MOUNTAIN OF ARTS & ENTERTAINMENT

"Worthy is the lamb that was slain to receive power and riches and wisdom and strength and honor and GLORY and blessing."
Revelation 5:12

Worthy is the lamb to receive glory! When we receive and model any of God's seven primary attributes of love we are, in essence, restoring His correct reputation on earth. He receives what we have become and displayed on earth. We are becoming back to God what He has provided for us and through us to others. The Greek word used here for glory is *Doxa.* This is the general word for glory, but glory itself is a word with a wide range of definitions that all convey something otherworldly. Ultimately, it's the wow factor of the divine and in this case specifically associated with His unparalleled creativity. In the

Old Testament, glory was a unique presence of God that could show up as fire, smoke, or a cloud. It was always a sign to people that something heavenly was happening. Glory was also meant to signify economic abundance and favor—all at a supernatural level.

God doesn't just love us in theory. His love is expressed in a nuanced way that is unique on each mountain. It is love in action and it expresses His genuine care for us through practical solutions in every area of our lives and our culture. On the Mountain of Arts & Entertainment God's love is seen as glory. God displays His love for us in His creation and through the glory of His creativity coming through us as His children. When we see the glory of His creativity, we encounter an aspect of who He is, and it reminds us that He not only exists, but that He loved us enough to give us beauty, humor, symmetry, design, and unfolding drama through what we wrongly refer to as "Mother Nature." When we experience the glory of creativity through others, we also encounter God as love. Habakkuk 2:14 tells us, "The knowledge of the glory of the Lord will cover the earth as the waters cover the sea." Perhaps no area of society is more set up for this than the Mountain of Arts & Entertainment.

This is the one area of society that intentionally sets up platforms where His glory was ultimately designed to shine—through His participating kids who understand the assignment to re-image Him in every area of society. God's true creativity lifts and inspires souls, as opposed to Satan's counterfeit creativity which is only capable of stirring up lust, perversion, fear, death, and violence. It only triumphs on the stage in the absence of our Creator's true glory. When we really begin to understand our assignment, we will partner with our Creator in wowing the world with His majestic splendor and glory in an explosion of unparalleled and unprecedented creative genius.

6. THE BIG LIE ABOUT GOD ON THE MOUNTAIN OF ARTS & ENTERTAINMENT:
GOD DOESN'T WANT US TO HAVE FUN

Every time we're exposed to the Mountain of Arts & Entertainment the enemy wants our takeaway to be, "The way I entertain myself is irrelevant to God because He's uninterested and too serious to have fun or care about my happiness."

The big lie about God that's currently being perpetuated about God on the

NOTES

Mountain of Arts & Entertainment is that God doesn't want us to have fun. This lie is built on another lie—that God Himself isn't fun because He's so holy and serious. That lie is built on yet another lie—that God can't have fun because He's so busy policing all our sins. We wrongly believe that if He can't enjoy us, then we have no right ourselves to enjoy things.

When we perceive God as distant and uninterested in our fun, in the context of arts and entertainment, we look like a bunch of children who had to sneak out of the house in the middle of the night in order to go have some real fun because our parents are too strict to allow us what we need. We need to have fun and feel happy as much as we need proper nutrition. We wither in every way without it. It literally affects our body, soul, and spirit when we go through life without enough fun—those things that make us feel happy.

God has clearly wired us for happiness. When we feel happy, certain chemicals and hormones are released in our bodies that are vital for mental and physical health. When we don't have them, we are depressed, and our bodies begin to make extra adrenaline until they can't anymore, causing illnesses and extreme fatigue. Once we believe we have a God who could not possibly enjoy creative and celebratory expressions than we unwittingly force a partnership with the counterfeit creativity that comes from teaming with Jezebel.

7. HOW THIS LIE ABOUT GOD ON THE MOUNTAIN OF ARTS & ENTERTAINMENT PLAYS OUT IN CULTURE

Arts and entertainment is the most influential sphere of culture of this age. We are most definitely an entertainment-dominant generation. When we incorrectly perceive that God doesn't want us to have fun and couldn't care less if we experience happiness in life, then we sing, write, create, and jest about things that further our belief that He either doesn't exist or doesn't care about us. Hearts that don't know their God cares about them do what any child does when he doesn't feel loved—they either try to get attention through destructive behavior, subconsciously daring their parents to intervene, or they simply disconnect their heart from the relationship. When we can't have what we value, we tend to protect our heart by no longer valuing that thing. If it's God's attention we value and need but can't seem to find, then, like a toddler, we create drama and chaos around us until He steps in to rescue us from ourselves and the destruction we've created. Or, we disconnect and distance our heart from God so that we don't have to face the disappointment we feel about our wrong perception of His heart toward us. Either way we choose to respond plays out in the art and entertainment outlets we've created. We sing, dance, and act out our pain and the rebellion it triggers in us, which continues promoting a false fantasy to the next generation. Generally speaking, with rare exceptions, celebrities end up promoting a destructive lifestyle as normal, healthy fun, when in reality it's born out of rejection and disappointment with God. That doesn't make their performances or life work inherently evil, but it's destructive in that what they do, say, or sing about lulls others into the false conclusions of their own broken hearts. They were given genuine gifts from God to express creativity and excellence through, but they found only a portion of their glory—their best broken self rather than their best healed self.

Like every other area of culture, this cycle continues to advance a lie about what God is really like. The next generation buys it, repackages it, and sells it again. When those who are in the arts and entertainment industry find the personal glory that God gave them coming from a healed perspective of God, they will feel validated and seen by Him as His son or daughter who is able to be enjoyed and delighted in. It will overflow into whatever their particular expression is and into their personal lifestyle as a celebrity, and it will help break the cycle we have become stuck in. They will create and compete in ways that cause us to believe God is near and He is good. It's not that their life's creative work won't be true-to-life and authentic, but the conclusions they lead us to will be life-giving.

8. THE BIG TRUTH ABOUT GOD ON THE MOUNTAIN OF ARTS & ENTERTAINMENT:
GOD WANTS US TO ENJOY LIFE!

To enjoy means to find pleasure in. God as Creator wants us to find pleasure in the midst of everyday life. Creativity that reflects Him and is a response to His love will provoke emotions in the observer that eventually lead to pleasure—something that pleases in the truest sense. Jesus said that the truth will set you free. When what we celebrate through art and entertainment is founded in the truth of who God is and how involved He is in our lives, then this area of culture will create freedom in the hearts of the ones being entertained—freedom, not addictions or bondage to perversions that leave us forever unsatisfied. Jesus described Satan as a thief who comes only to steal, kill, and destroy. Unfortunately, we often partner with this enemy without realizing it and become instruments of pillage, death, and destruction through the very area we were meant to display love and life as we discover our personal glory. Jesus went on to say that He came to give us life abundantly. That means fullness of life to such a degree that it goes beyond what we need or require. It is extravagant living that He offers us.

Jesus wasn't talking about some "hide from the scary world because it might taint us" kind of living—nor did He live that way Himself. We must stop pointing fingers of judgment at those in the entertainment industry because we haven't offered them a better way of creativity. We've refused to bless and make room for the creativity God wanted to pour through them because it looked different than the boxes we made for them in the four walls of the church. Much of what comes out of Hollywood is indeed toxic, but a lot is truly amazing and inspiring. The enemy of God loves it when we accuse one another and miss out on each other's strengths, furthering his destructive patterns in our lives—our bondage to religion and Hollywood's bondage to perversion. It's all the same in the eyes of the One who made us all to be free. God wants us free from religion and free from perversion. Whatever someone is in bondage to produces the same result—art and entertainment that is absent of light.

Nothing thrives the way it was meant to apart from light. Christians must admit our part in the current broken state of the entertainment industry.

Our God is a celebrating God. He loves celebrating. He loves His kids celebrating. He loves parties, dramas, music, dance, humor, and feasting. Even in the Old Testament, God commanded Israel to have seven feasts for every one fast. The truth is, not only does God want us to have fun, but He insists on it. It is essential kingdom-of-God DNA. The kingdom of God is righteousness, peace, and joy in the Holy Spirit. Joy is not foolishness per se, but it's definitely heavenly merriment. When the Holy Spirit first showed up, an explanation had to be made about His unprecedented presence and its effect on those in the upper room. To the degree we have carried a God who is decidedly serious and drab—to that degree we haven't yet picked up on who He is but are in fact under the lie of the enemy that presents itself as the counterfeit knowledge of who God is.

9. OUR ASSURANCE ON THE MOUNTAIN OF ARTS & ENTERTAINMENT: YOU ARE ENJOYED

When the face of God as Creator is correctly displayed as Glory on the Mountain of Arts & Entertainment it assures us that we all are enjoyed by the

One who made us, and we can therefore enjoy Him and life itself to the fullest.

God actually enjoys us and all the things that make us different from others. When we're convinced that God enjoys us just like we are, then we are free to enjoy ourselves too. God has given us permission to have fun, enjoy life, and celebrate the glory He put in others and in the things around us because He does.

10. PARTNER WITH GOD AS CREATOR ON THE MOUNTAIN OF ARTS & ENTERTAINMENT

To properly fulfill our assignment on the Mountain of Arts & Entertainment we must truly know God as Creator ourselves, learn to reflect who He is as Creator personally, and then connect it to the way we create and entertain others with our talent. We must become experts on this aspect of God's love and then give it away to all who are influenced by our role on this mountain.

A REFORMER'S ASSIGNMENT ON THE MOUNTAIN OF ARTS & ENTERTAINMENT:

1. Carry a hunger to know the heart of God as Creator in your own life so that you can bring it into your professional role in an authentic way. What you contend for personally will easily overflow from you in the workplace. Ask God to reveal His creativity to and through you.

2. Understand that fun that leaves us short or long term damaged in any way is abuse and should not be considered entertainment.

3. Use this question to determine if you are truly helping restore the glory of God to arts and entertainment: What am I promoting to the hearts of those I am entertaining through what I've created?

4. Determine if you're displaying the light of God and His heart of love and true freedom through your influence, or are you promoting bondage to perversion, addictions, and darkness? Truly there is no neutral ground.

5. Don't feel like what you create must be directly about or connected to God or religion, but know that if your passion is for art, entertainment, or sports,

you carry great responsibility and accountability for what you promote in all you do and in your lifestyle. The world is literally watching as you perform for an audience of One.

6. While pursuing excellence in your area of talent, remember to prioritize excellence of character in terms of lifestyle, authenticity, relationships, and service.

7. If you are called to the Mountain of Arts & Entertainment, your ultimate mission is to model the greater creativity that comes only from God and prophesy His heart for humanity through it.

8. If what you do "creatively" erodes societal moral fabric, then it truly is the counterfeit. If what you do serves to lift the people's spirits by at least indirectly pointing them to the truth about what God is really like, then you have found real creativity and the genuine glory you were made to live from. You are then co-laboring with God the Creator and are a minister with a platform and pulpit that is more powerful and influential than those found in most churches.

9. Know that if you do not participate in arts and entertainment God's better way, Satan looks for every opportunity to use you as a pawn and eventually make you another one of his casualties on this mountain.

10. Do not allow the spirit of Jezebel, through people, to prostitute the gifts God has given you. When He promotes you, you won't have to compromise to remain there.

11. If you are called to the entertainment industry, then the glory of God was meant to be seen on you. It's not wrong to be spotlighted—only wrong to keep that glory and not genuinely give it back to Him, acknowledging it was all through Him and to Him.

12. Don't copy or repackage someone else's creativity just for the possibility of success. Go to God Himself who has limitless creativity and ask Him for creativity and abilities that have never been seen on earth, and you'll experience greater true success than you can imagine. Be willing to spend

time in His presence accessing the sounds, music, fashion, etc. that He's made available for you and for this generation.

Reformers who have the privilege of affecting the masses through creativity will steward well over their influence, using it to promote directly or indirectly the true heart of God for the world. They will use the truth they have discovered about God's goodness and power to overcome every lie and teach the next generation how to live authentic lives with God in the center of relationships in a real and non-religious way. Many currently in the industry will have radical conversion experiences with God and will no longer be ashamed to go to Him as their Source. They will extravagantly use their wealth to bring creative solutions to the worst problems on the globe and want no credit for it. They will weep at award ceremonies because of the presence of God as Creator among them.

The new levels of creativity and success will manifest not through those who sold their souls to make it big, but through those who enjoy life from a position of true freedom and have learned to co-labor with God the Creator. They will not be motivated by money and fame but will indeed make great sums of money and carry fame that doesn't change them or push them to compromise. Their chief concern will be God's fame and the privilege of doing their part to love and uplift society by displaying His love and glory. A great up-lifting of society will come out of what God begins to release through this mountain. Society will learn that everything from heaven is better! Better outcomes and better products come from heaven. Our Creator wants to reveal to us just how fun He is!

FOR MORE IN-DEPTH INFORMATION ON THESE TOPICS IN OUR OTHER RESOURCES:

The Seven Mountain Prophecy (Ch 10, Overview)

The Seven Mountain Mantle (Ch 17)

The Seven Mountain Mandate Video Course and Workbook (Session 8)

Rainbow God: The Seven Colors of Love (Ch 9)

Rainbow God Video Course and Workbook (Session 4)

The Seven Mountain Renaissance (Ch 11)

GOD AS CREATOR

My sons and daughters made in My image, how beautiful and perfect you are—each carrying enough of Me, enough of My glory to stun those who can see with awe and amazement. Even in the weakest, most marred version of who you are, you are My delight—a wonder and an inspiration to My heart. I love it when you're free, really free to be you and to shine with what I've put in you. All the things that make you, you, are endearing to Me. I love it when you enjoy Me, but I especially love it when you enjoy yourself, when you enjoy each other, and when you enjoy life and all that I created for you and all that I've created with you. Could you dare to believe that, right in this very moment, I enjoy you more than you've ever enjoyed anything or anyone in your lifetime? Could you dare to believe that I truly enjoy you?

I created you with a glory all your own. I want you to love yourself because I'm in you—in every cell and behind every sustaining breath. I'm in your potential and I am in your now. I'm the artist who sees you as the perfect expression on the canvas that is you. I'm the sculptor who sees you as the intricate masterpiece hewn from the rock that is you. I'm the storyteller who's writing your beautiful and victorious story into the pages of time. I'm the chef who sees all the flavors that are you and is fusing it all together until you become a feast for the eyes of eternity. I'm the coach who sees you as the one with just the right strength and determination to make this legendary game into a victorious finish that will be spoken of for all eternity.

I am your Creator and I created you with a glory all your own, as well as with a desire to look for and enjoy the glory that is Me in others. I give you permission to live life to the fullest while you're discovering all that I am and everywhere that I can be seen. I give you permission to find the glory that I've put in you and in others and celebrate it with Me!

Profits are
the applause you get
for taking care
of your people.

—Ken Blanchard

CHAPTER SIX

THE MOUNTAIN OF ECONOMY

In the area of culture referred to as ECONOMY, we see God as PROVIDER, the color GREEN. He is LOVE displayed as RICHES. These are the riches of God's love expressed as the abundance of resources through our economy. Our world economic system was meant to reflect the heart of God as our Provider, and when it does, we will know it because there will be no lack. To the degree that love, as riches, is poured out as practical resources and basic needs are met for quality of life for all of humanity, we can know that God is involved in our economy—whether it's our personal, national, or global economic status. Satan uses the principality MAMMON (GREED) and the demonic strategy of the CANAANITES (LOVE OF MONEY) to distort the truth of who God is. God has given us a mighty archangel, ZERACHIEL, to fight for those called to this mountain. The LIE being perpetuated about God in our current ECONOMIC SYSTEM is: IT'S POINTLESS TO TRUST GOD FOR OUR RICHES. The TRUTH that we will learn to display in ECONOMY is: GOD ENJOYS PROVIDING FOR US AND THROUGH US.

1. THE CANAANITES AND THE PRINCIPALITY MAMMON: THE DEMONIC STRATEGY ON THE MOUNTAIN OF ECONOMY

The word Canaanite means *merchant* or *trader* and its etymology is from a word meaning both *zealous* as well as *brought low*. It speaks of the enemy's strategy to use *greed* on the Mountain of Economy/Business to ultimately bring people and their nation's economy down.

The CANAANITES were one of the seven nations the Israelites had to conquer in order to obey God and take their promised land. They represent the love of money and the demons of greed that operate on the Mountain of Economy, as well as the strategy to convince people that money is their true source of provision.

MAMMON is Satan's illegal principality on the Mountain of Economy. His name means a*varice* or *extreme greed*. Jesus said, "You cannot serve both God and Mammon." (Mt. 6:24) The demonic strategy is to fill society with people who look to money rather than God as their source of provision, continuing the cycle of broken economic systems that are rooted in greed rather than a trust in God as Provider. Mammon subtly and deceitfully competes for the throne of God in our lives and says, "I am your source." Mammon shows up as extreme capitalism without guardrails. Mammon exalts an aggressive lifestyle of leveraging every minute, every person, and every opportunity for the ultimate purpose of making more money. It masks as stewardship, but only stewards the pursuit of money. Mammon is illustratively like the slot machines of Vegas. It may give you some early returns, but then crashes you into poverty because it's not the way we were designed by God to make wealth.

People who work in business and influence the economic system are not the enemy. Even the most greedy and corrupt are not the problem. They are often partnering with Satan and the demonic realm without realizing it. The true enemy is Satan, the father of lies, who doesn't want us to live free from greed because, when we do, we'll discover the generous heart of God as Provider who loves to provide for us and through us for others. Satan tries to get us out of balance in one way or another, either by pushing us to pursue money too much or convincing us to settle for poverty. He'll actually help us make money to keep us always wanting more. He enslaves us to a fear of losing everything, provoking us to hoard in dread of a disaster. He does whatever it takes to keep us stressed, worried, and always focused on money. We end up disconnected from trusting in God who not only has all wealth, but can create wealth and riches out of nothing.

Mammon's Strategy:

1. Prevent the face of God as Provider from being restored to society.
2. Prevent humanity from having access to the truth of how God loves us through the way He provides riches and abundance of resources through our economy.
3. Prevent people from knowing that God enjoys providing riches for us and through us.
4. Prevent people from experiencing a healed perspective of the goodness of God through the Mountain of Economy, a mountain ultimately meant to assure us that God is generous and has provision for us.

2. THE ARCHANGEL ZERACHIEL FIGHTS ON THE MOUNTAIN OF ECONOMY

ZERACHIEL means "provided or sent by God" — His name reveals His assignment which is to assist in restoring the image of God in the earth as Provider.

Zerachiel and his host of angel armies serve the Lord of Hosts by helping the sons and daughters of God who are called to impact the Mountain of Economy. They are focused on assisting current and future ministers of wealth in their positions among the nations as conduits for resourcing kingdom solutions that ultimately display God's generous heart as Provider. Zerachiel fights with us to overcome the demonic realm by making sure that those who put their trust in God have favor and opportunities to discover finances and resources.

3. THE FACE OF GOD AS PROVIDER ON THE MOUNTAIN OF ECONOMY

Mammon gets overthrown when the lie behind Mammon gets overthrown by the truth of who God is as Provider. As we look at this aspect of God we see another beautiful face of the godhead. We remember that one of His primary names is Jehovah-Jireh, the God who is provision itself. From Genesis to Revelation we are shown a Provider God who delights in giving generously. He shared with Adam and Eve His abundance of fruit trees He had provided for them. He promised and gave Abraham abundance of wealth. He enticed the children of Israel to their Promised Land by telling them of the abundance of everything good that they would find there. Throughout the Old Testament those who loved and trusted Him found themselves overflowing in abundance of provision.

In the New Testament through the person of Jesus He continued to reveal His generous heart. Jesus' first miracle was a provision miracle to make a wedding successful even though no actual ministry was taking place. He provided 180 gallons of the best wine that shocked the master of ceremonies who had never seen such a thing. Jesus provided more than enough for Peter's taxes, more than enough for over 5,000 hungry people, more than enough for the disciples who had been fishing all night and catching nothing. God clearly loves to provide extravagantly and abundantly.

NOTES

It becomes imperative for those who are called to the Mountain of Economy to understand and reveal who He is as Provider. The assignment on every mountain is to reveal Him as He is highlighted in that mountain and in doing so the enemy gets knocked out, the people rejoice, and the glory of God gets revealed. Mammon is powerful in this area of society only for lack of a proper demonstration by God's kids of what His capabilities are. The foundation of our assignment here is to reveal the extravagant generosity and kindness of our God for every kind of human situation that requires funding. He doesn't just fund ministry. He funds marriages, taxes, fishing, picnics and every other kind of need. The kingdom encompasses ministry assignments but also the other parts of our life. God cares about everything and He will provide abundantly for everything, if we can believe that about Him and come to Him for all of our provision needs. He's always looking for joyous, trusting, risking children to be His ministers of wealth on the earth.

4. THE COLOR GREEN ON THE MOUNTAIN OF ECONOMY

Green is the color associated with the Mountain of Economy because it reminds us of growth and prosperity. Even U.S. dollars are called green-backs. When something is green-lighted, we think of moving forward. Of course, in recent years, the expression "Go Green" reminds us to value the life and resources on our planet enough to conserve them. Our Provider is the source of all we value and of life itself. Green is another color of His love that our economy could use more of.

In chromotherapy, the study and science of healing through colors, it has been identified that the color green may relax nerves and assist the body as an antiseptic against harmful micro-organisms. It only makes sense that when our spirit knows it's been provided for by God, it puts us at peace, strengthening our body's defense against harmful lies from the enemy that would tempt us to believe He can't be trusted to provide for us individually, as well as collectively as nations.

5. GOD'S LOVE DISPLAYED AS RICHES ON THE MOUNTAIN OF ECONOMY

> *"Worthy is the lamb that was slain to receive power*
> *and RICHES and wisdom and strength and*
> *honor and glory and blessing."*
> ***Revelation 5:12***

Worthy is the Lamb to receive riches! When we receive and model any of God's seven primary attributes of love we are in essence restoring His correct reputation on earth. He receives what we have become and displayed on earth. We are becoming back to God what He has provided for us and through us to others.

God doesn't just love us in theory. His love is expressed in a nuanced way that is unique on each mountain. It is love in action and it expresses His genuine care for us through practical solutions in every area of our lives and our culture. On the Mountain of Economy God's love is experienced as riches.

When love is communicated through provision it registers on the heart of the recipient as riches and wealth in the truest sense. The Greek word for riches is *plutos,* where the word plutocracy comes from. It means "fullness of wealth, possessions, money, abundance, richness and valuable bestowment." This is an aspect of the nature of God as Provider.

God's love is so limitless that it overflows everywhere things are done His way. For those who have hearts to let Him in, there's always plenty of love. When business is done God's way, His love overflows as riches, and there's plenty to go around. His love in our economic culture overflows as God our Provider. What does God provide for us? Nothing less than the riches of His love. Love looks like riches when displayed in a nation's economy. God's love is meant to be displayed as riches, or the abundance of resources, through our economy. His love searches out all the things that keep us from knowing Him as Provider, and when we get His heart, we will do the same for others.

6. THE BIG LIE ABOUT GOD ON THE MOUNTAIN OF ECONOMY: IT'S POINTLESS TO TRUST GOD FOR RICHES OR PROVISION

Every time we're exposed to the Mountain of Economy, the enemy wants our takeaway to be, "The only way for me to have enough is to count on my

NOTES

own ability to accumulate finances and resources. God doesn't get involved in everyday money matters, so I have to figure it out myself. He may sometimes help with basic needs, but He certainly wouldn't help me nor is He ok with abundant riches."

The big lie about God that's currently being perpetuated about Him on the Mountain of Economy—that it's pointless to trust God for riches or provision—literally steals from God's children. Furthermore, it's why we fall into alignment with Mammon and choose his method of fear and greed. We're filled with fear under the weight of finding and/or keeping the riches that we need, so then a strategy of greed is seen as the answer. When provision is abundant through greed, then we have a feeling of euphoria and invincibility. It gives steroids to pride and independence. When provision is scarce, there is fear and anxiety—as a whispering enemy is faithful to be telling us all the worst-case scenarios that are about to happen.

Proverbs tells us that the financial blessing of the Lord adds no sorrow with it. When we are convinced He indeed does provide for us, it registers as peace and trust. When wealth has been gained through extreme self-effort and greed, there's no amount of riches that satisfies the heart and sorrow certainly follows. An orphan spirit always fears losing everything. Sons and daughters are secured in their hearts regardless of their bank account size. They are secured by their personal revelation of God's heart of provision towards them—knowing who He is and how He is becomes their anchor. The lie that fear and greed build into the foundations of our hearts and our economic systems is torn down when a solution from God is discovered, promoted, financed, and implemented.

7. HOW THIS LIE ABOUT GOD ON THE MOUNTAIN OF ECONOMY PLAYS OUT IN CULTURE

When we don't believe we can trust God for what we need, we revert back to what we unfortunately learned in school—depend on yourself and don't count on anyone else. With that mentality comes a whole skill set of using and climbing over anyone necessary to make your way to success. Individuals do it and corporations do it. The unspoken rules are the same, and the eyes become trained to see others as a means to an end and definitely not the way God sees us or desires us to see one another.

Mammon competes for the place of preeminence in our life. When we give ourselves permission to be lovers of money, we set ourselves up to resent God. When we find our security in our bank account, we make that our trust fund rather than making God the Provider our trust. No matter what financial gain you attain, if it lessens your trust in God, it's your enemy and not your friend. Many of us require a daily recommitment to God in this area with some practical proofs such as giving first to God and then becoming committed to ongoing generosity with the rest.

8. THE BIG TRUTH ABOUT GOD ON THE MOUNTAIN OF ECONOMY: GOD ENJOYS PROVIDING RICHES FOR US AND THROUGH US

God loves providing, without an agenda, just because He's kind and this is His very nature. As it relates to society, He's not bartering their souls for provision. He doesn't require that anyone become born again and fully serve Him to provide for them. He loves to do it just because He loves all His sons and daughters, even if they don't yet know to love Him back.

God as our Provider is not Santa Claus, content to be visited once a year with our laundry list of needs. Neither is He a gum-ball machine we can put a little something in and get out what we want. God is also not like a mafia boss that we need to pay off with an offering so that He won't break our kneecaps. He is much more relational and generous than we can imagine. He has literally provided for every possible need we will ever have emotionally, physically, monetarily, and spiritually. But it doesn't stop there—as One who is bigger than time itself, He has gone into our eternity and already prepared for all we will need there too. We see in every area of culture that God provides Himself and His better plans as the cure. He has even provided us with love, so we can have love to give back to Him!

Because we are made in God's image, we were also created to provide riches and resources for others. It all starts with recognizing who He is as Provider and inviting Him into all decisions regarding anything with money or business. All who want to serve as an extension of His provision on earth are invited to participate. He doesn't require you to be perfect or have a high paying job. You may never be able to build enough trust in Him to administer billions, but maybe you can handle hundreds or thousands. You can start where you are and see what you are able to grow into. Our working currency is a simple trust in God that is earned as we learn to be faithful in the little. As you establish your identity as one who seeks first His kingdom with the small amounts you steward over, you can then grow into greater measures of stewardship of riches that bring a blessing to the giver and the receivers.

9. OUR ASSURANCE ON THE MOUNTAIN OF ECONOMY: GOD HAS PROVISION FOR YOU

When the face of God as Provider is correctly displayed as riches on the Mountain of Economy, it assures us that God has provision for us personally and as a society.

God can and wants to take care of all of that we need and our quality of life, especially as it relates to where we live, what we eat, and our physical appearance. He's happy to supply more than enough for our needs and those we are responsible for. He wants to help us be successful financially in the assignments He's given us and empower us to supply more than enough for others out of our abundance.

10. PARTNER WITH GOD AS PROVIDER ON THE MOUNTAIN OF ECONOMY

In order to properly fulfill our assignment on the Mountain of Economy we must truly know God as Provider ourselves, learn to reflect who He is as Provider personally, and then connect it to the way we make all of our financial decisions that lead to potential riches. We must become experts on this aspect of God's love and then give it away to all who are influenced by our role on this mountain.

A REFORMER'S ASSIGNMENT ON THE MOUNTAIN OF ECONOMY

1. Carry a trusting heart towards God as your Provider and a generous heart towards others in your personal life so that you can bring it into your professional role in a genuine way. What you contend for personally will easily overflow from you in the workplace. Ask God to reveal His true heart towards you: "Remember that it is the Lord your God who gives you the power to gain wealth…" Deuteronomy 8:18

2. Don't feel that God will only bless you as you finance things connected to religion. Anytime you use your economic ability to finance practical solutions that meet needs with authenticity and excellence, it has the potential to registers on person's heart as God Himself caring for them—at least on a subconscious level.

3. Steward well over your talent and ability to discover and transfer wealth into kingdom purposes. Remember that sometimes kingdom purposes aren't obvious in a direct way.

4. You must cultivate trust in your relationship with God, just like you do in any important relationship in your life. God's currency is trust and the enemy's currency is fear, greed, or both. If you find your daily realities being more in the fear/greed category, then make the necessary adjustments. Trust isn't easy, but it's necessary. Sometimes you have to stare down your fear and eyeball it face to face and declare to it and to yourself that you trust God the Provider. God is not fragile, but our trust can be. One bad day for Wall Street and our confidence can come crashing down.

5. Don't spend the majority of your life doing something you hate doing. Your work was meant to be your life's calling that produces in you a servant-hearted passion. You can only find your purpose and fulfillment when you are sincerely motivated to make the world a better place by accessing and releasing His kingdom. Your vocation is the exchange of finances for service provided. Your ultimate goal in business should be to be so passionate about the humanitarian value of what you do, that your work-life reflects an image of God.

6. Don't just work hard, believe hard. There is a level of provision that comes from working hard, but greater provision is yet to be accessed when we believe in God as a faithful Provider and partner in all we do.

7. You must ascend the Mountain of Economy in the opposite spirit of greed. As a kingdom citizen wealth is never the end goal. This separates us from wealth-pursuers outside of the context of the kingdom context—for them it's all about the accumulation of wealth. For a citizen of the kingdom, wealth is that favor which allows one to best fulfill their heavenly assignment.

8. Know that you are always loved, but favor comes and goes. You are loved even when you don't see favor in your finances. Favor is always for the assignment. When you are ready for the assignment and the assignment is ready for you, the favor will be there.

9. Live with the conviction that anything is possible. Jesus said that it was more difficult for a rich man to enter the kingdom of heaven than for a camel to go through the eye of a needle, but then He went on to say that with God all things are possible. This tells us that becoming rich is fraught with many traps and dangers that most fall into, but He does have inheritance for us. The test is to stay dependent and trusting in Him and not in what He is providing.

10. Understand that God wants us to experience wealth and abundance, but He wants it clear to our souls that He sourced it. We must have intentionally brought Him into all processes having to do with gaining finances or riches so that when we experience prosperity we give Him the glory and we don't exhaust ourselves in our own strength in our future endeavors.

11. Invite God into every financial decision and deal you make. Obey what He tells you even if it seems counter intuitive, and seek His wisdom above anything else. Mammon's system is to leverage every financial opportunity. God's system is to radically give and obey at every opportunity.

12. Don't just make a goal for how much income you can accumulate; make your primary goal to see how much you can give away. Be a channel, not a dam. Ministers of wealth will have such a profound, trusting relationship with God that they will always know that more is forthcoming when what they do is connected to the issues that touch His heart.

13. Never be intimidated as a believer in the financial industry. Bring His heart as Provider with you into board rooms of companies and corporations. God always has the better ways of doing things with better outcomes, and He loves to reveal them through you.

There is no economic crisis on earth that God has not already placed the solution for in His sons and daughters who are willing to co-labor with Him.

There is no economic crisis that will ever come that He won't already have the solution for, available through His kids. We simply need to awaken to who He is and what He is all about and then arise and shine with what He has given us. We must become convinced that we have never been orphaned on planet earth, no matter how much it may feel that way at times. God knows the things we need, and He has given us the parameters of how we are to receive His abundant provision in a way that it won't harm us. He gave us clear instructions to seek His kingdom first, and then He will give all that's needed to us and through us. The current economic crisis in any nation is never hopeless.

FOR MORE IN-DEPTH INFORMATION ON THESE TOPICS IN OUR OTHER RESOURCES:

The Seven Mountain Prophecy (Ch 8, Overview)

The Seven Mountain Mantle (Ch 15)

The Seven Mountain Mandate Video Course and Workbook (Session 3)

Rainbow God: The Seven Colors of Love (Ch 8)

Rainbow God Video Course and Workbook (Session 5)

The Seven Mountain Renaissance (Ch 9)

GOD AS PROVIDER

My sons and daughters, I never grow weary of caring for you—of being your source when you allow Me to be. I know it's hard to trust Me because it's hard to know what's your part and what's My part. But know this—I get it. I know what it's like to learn how to be responsible and also childlike and trusting. I taught Jesus how and I can teach you too. But remember, it requires constant communication and constant checking in with Me, which of course I like.

I know it's hard for you, but I like it when you're absolutely in need of Me for everything that you need in life. I like it when you notice how I provide for you, but even when you don't, I'll keep providing for you because that's who I am. Of course, there are times it doesn't look like I'm providing for you or for the nations and it looks like I don't care, but that simply isn't true. The proof that I care is that you care. Can you look at a child who doesn't have enough or the basic needs of life and not care? Do you enjoy giving your children more than enough and extravagantly blessing them? Do you feel proud and content when your children share what you've given them and give extravagantly to others? Of course, you care! That's because you're Mine, made in My image.

When there's lack and you think I don't care and you think I'm not going to provide for you—just ask yourself what you would do for your child. That's My heart. Now does that mean you'll always see My provision played out in an obvious way? As you know, it doesn't because I'm also providing for you riches that cannot be taken from you. And those can only be gained in the places of contradiction and seeming lack. Even when evil comes and kills, steals, and destroys—it's not because it just slipped past Me or my account was too low.

Everyone who looks to Me, who allows Me to provide whatever it is that's needed—finds it in Me, whether now or in My presence in eternity. I am Your source and I love providing for you and through you all the riches of who I am and what I have, in My perfect way and in My perfect time. Come to Me, I'm all you need. Don't ever be afraid to ask, to trust, and to wait. Don't ever be afraid to give—and know that when you're generous with your riches, I love to trust you to be generous with Mine.

What you think
about God is the
most important thing
about you.

— A.W. Tozer

CHAPTER SEVEN

THE MOUNTAIN OF RELIGION

In the area of culture referred to as RELIGION, we see God as REDEEMER, the color BLUE. He is LOVE displayed as HONOR. This is the honor that shows God authentic reverence, value, and deep respect, which is far from simply following religious rules or behaving out of obligation and performance. Honor, through religion, was meant to be infused into how we not only live towards Him but towards others as well. Satan uses THE RELIGIOUS SPIRIT (FALSE WORSHIP) and the demonic strategy of the PERIZZITES (IDOLATRY) to distort the truth of who God is. God has given us a mighty archangel, MICHAEL, to fight for those called to this mountain. The LIE being perpetuated about God in the current RELIGIOUS SYSTEM is: WE HAVE TO WORK HARD AND BE GOOD IN ORDER TO KNOW GOD. The TRUTH about God that we will learn to display in RELIGION is: WE NEED A REDEEMER IN ORDER TO KNOW GOD.

1. THE PERIZZITES AND THE RELIGIOUS SPIRIT: THE DEMONIC STRATEGY ON THE MOUNTAIN OF RELIGION

The word Perizzite means *unwalled rural dwelling place* and it represents the lack of protection brought on by idolatry and false worship on the Mountain of Religion.

The PERIZZITES were one of the seven nations that the Israelites had to conquer in order to obey God and take their promised land. They represent a work of idolatry strategically designed to bring people and people groups under the dominion of religiosity.

THE RELIGIOUS SPIRIT is Satan's illegal principality on the Mountain of Religion and very likely his strongest alter ego. It represents *false worship*. As Lucifer, Satan was the most intimate with what true worship looks like which is why the demonic strategy is to steal worship that belongs only to God. The religious spirit will always prioritize secondary matters over heart matters and rituals over relationship.

People who claim there is no God or who hate Christians or believe different than you do are not the enemy. Satan is the only true enemy on the Mountain of Religion, just as he is on all of the other mountains. He saw our tendency as humans to reach out to our Creator for relationship and pushed us past the simplicity of true intimacy and into religion. In essence, Satan took our right to have a real relationship with our Father and deceived us into exchanging it for religion based on knowing principles rather than the freedom to know God Himself. Like every other good thing God has offered us, Satan offers a counterfeit. Religion, by definition, is a way of belief or worship. False religion is a set of rules or a system to follow in order to appease God. True religion is relationship, trust, and intimacy with God. There is one enemy in the war over religion. Any religion that teaches its followers to look at anyone other than Satan himself as the enemy is a false religion. Because humans are the common denominator of all religions, you can be sure that all religions are guilty of pointing fingers at other people as the enemy rather than at the true source of all darkness. Yes, we can align ourselves knowingly or unknowingly with that one enemy, but ultimately even the most evil person on the planet is not the enemy but simply his pawn.

The Strategy of the Religious Spirit:
1. Prevent the face of God as Redeemer from being restored to society.
2. Prevent humanity from having access to the truth of how God loves us through the ways He honors us.
3. Prevent people from knowing that we don't have to work hard and be good in order to know God, we simply need Jesus as our Redeemer.
4. Prevent people from experiencing a healed perspective of the goodness of God through the Mountain of Religion, which was ultimately meant to provide for and assure us of our eternal security.

2. THE ARCHANGEL MICHAEL FIGHTS ON THE MOUNTAIN OF RELIGION

MICHAEL means "Who is like God?" — His name reveals his assignment which is to assist in restoring the image of God in the earth as Redeemer.

As the one assigned to advance and protect a people who look like God, Michael has been the most loyal from the very beginning. The glory he carries is so magnificent, if we could see him, it could make some wrongly think that he's God Himself. Michael and his host of angel armies serve the Lord of Hosts by guarding Israel (as Jerusalem is the geographical religious capital of the world) and by helping the sons and daughters of God who are called to impact the Mountain of Religion. Michael and the angels with him are focused on our mission to partner with the Holy Spirit to bring the revelation to the world that we don't have to earn salvation or work hard and behave to know God because He has provided Jesus as our Redeemer.

3. THE FACE OF GOD AS REDEEMER ON THE MOUNTAIN OF RELIGION

A redeemer is one who gains possession by payment or ransom. It's the payment for a prisoner. We all came from the heart of God before He put us on earth, but we're born lost and in need of being ransomed. All have sinned, and it's sin that separates us from the privilege of living eternally with God. God the Redeemer, in His wonderful mercy, came in the person of Jesus Christ. God loved the world so much that He gave His only Son as a gift of righteousness to "whosoever will." For the joy set before Him, He endured the cross and was willingly sacrificed. It is in Jesus that we see the perfect reflection of this face of God as Redeemer. This is the greatest love possible that the Godhead could possibly reveal to us. Greater love has no one than to lay His life down for another.

The risk and sacrifice of the Godhead was enormous as they allowed Jesus, God in the flesh, to be mistreated, misunderstood, mocked, betrayed and ultimately killed—so that we might have the right and privilege of a close relationship with the God of the Universe. He didn't just die so we could go to heaven. He died so that we might have close relationship with Him. He didn't just need companionship, or He would have kept the angels. He wanted close relational communion with that which was made in His image. He made us capable of experiencing depths of Him that even the angels were not wired to be able to experience. We must never forget that this is who God is as Redeemer.

We've celebrated this aspect of who our Savior is so much, that we've preached and lived as though this were all He is. Amazingly, despite the centrality of the message of the cross and the place of Jesus as our Redeemer, we as the Body of Christ seem to forget our assignment on this mountain. At times, it seems we believe Christianity to be the best religion to help people behave and stop all their sinning. We seem to forget to champion Jesus—not just as the original Redeemer through a transaction of "getting saved," but also as the ongoing Source and Fountain for all levels of redemption. He didn't die just so we could start behaving and go to heaven, but so that we might have relationship with Him now (not relationship with a religion or rules). In whatever ways we have each failed in our own righteousness, we can come boldly before His throne of grace clothed in Jesus' righteousness.

God as Redeemer is worthy of being truly understood so that we seek to establish this relational priority between God and the sons and daughters who don't yet acknowledge Him. He's looking for relationship, not behavior. Relationship will then engender the correct royal behavior. He isn't just trying to get a people to behave civilly. He's wants us to behave royally. That only truly happens when you know your true royalty because you're intimate enough with God to know and believe your true identity.

4. THE COLOR BLUE ON THE MOUNTAIN OF RELIGION

Blue is the color connected to the Mountain of Religion. It's associated with truth, revelation, and by extension the Holy Spirit. When you look up into the sky as high as you can, or as deep in the ocean as you can, you see blue. We are constantly surrounded, from the heights to the depths, by this color of God as Redeemer.

In chromotherapy, the study and science of healing through colors, it has been identified that the color blue is said to lubricate the joints and connective tissue as well as regulate the circulatory system. These are all things related to connectivity, which is what the Holy Spirit does for us as He connects us to Jesus, to each other in the Body of Christ, and then finally to society.

5. GOD'S LOVE DISPLAYED AS HONOR ON THE MOUNTAIN OF RELIGION

"Worthy is the lamb that was slain to receive power
and riches and wisdom and strength and
HONOR and glory and blessing."
Revelation 5:12

Worthy is the Lamb to receive honor! When we receive and model any of God's seven primary attributes of love we are, in essence, restoring His correct reputation on earth. He receives what we have become and displayed on earth. We are becoming back to God what He has provided for us and through us to others.

God doesn't just love us in theory. His love is expressed in a nuanced way that is unique on each mountain. It is love in action and it expresses His genuine care for us through practical solutions in every area of our lives and our culture. On the Mountain of Religion God's love is experienced as honor. When love is communicated through religion it registers on the heart of the recipient as honor. The Greek word used here in the original is *Time* (pronounced Tee-May). This word essentially means "the value, esteem or honor due someone for a price they paid." This of course speaks of Jesus and the honor due Him for the extreme price He paid for us on the cross. To confess Jesus as Savior above all else is the only true way to show Him the honor He is worthy of.

The Mountain of Religion is ultimately going to be a mountain that fully honors Jesus. This means that what will be restored to both society and to God, when He is received as Redeemer, is honor. Serving God on the Mountain of Religion is all about showcasing honor. It was so honorable the way Jesus came among us. He didn't come forcing religion down our throats but offered the free gift of salvation. He came as a reconciler between man and God rather than an enforcer of judgment. We must remember that so that we re-image Him properly. We were all deserving of maximum judgment, but He went one step lower—making eternal salvation 99.9% His effort and our .1% being to just say yes! He so desired to be known and related to that the limited requirements of the 10 Commandments were further reduced to, "Will you accept the free gift of righteousness?" What an honorable proposal!

As we advance our assignment on this Mountain of Religion, going up against the other false religions and idols that compete for the heart of God, we must advance as He modeled. The way is simultaneously very narrow and immensely wide. Jesus is the only door to eternal salvation and life in eternity with the Father. That's the narrowness of it, but the incredible width of it is that it's that simple. It's not Jesus plus the 10 Commandments...plus "be ye Holy as I am Holy." It's just Jesus. Romans 10:13 says God boiled redemption down to "whoever calls upon the name of the Lord will be saved." John

3:16 says, "For God so loved the world He gave His only son that whoever believes in Him will not perish but have eternal life." That's why there is such a severe consequence to saying no to that offer. The dishonor is just too great. It's the most dishonorable thing imaginable for One who gave everything on our behalf. Hebrews 2:3 says, "How shall we escape if we neglect so great a salvation." If the idea of hell is hard to stomach, it truly is the just reward for dishonoring this level of sacrifice.

When we see and understand the honorable example of our Redeemer, we see that the kingdom of God can never be advanced through imposition or force. Heaven operates under the bounds and constraints of voluntary honor. It's no longer fear of God that constrains. It's the honor of God that constrains. We will enjoy worshipping Him over and over and over again, not because Michael the archangel is prodding us, but because it will be the only satisfying thing we can do as our awareness of the honor due Him is clearly evidenced.

6. THE BIG LIE ABOUT GOD ON THE MOUNTAIN OF RELIGION: WE HAVE TO WORK HARD AND BE GOOD IN ORDER TO KNOW GOD

Every time we're exposed to the Mountain of Religion, the enemy wants our takeaway to be, "If having a relationship with God means I have to be good enough, then why even try? No matter how hard I work, I never really feel close to Him. Honestly, can anyone really be sure of where they will go after they die? Maybe there are many ways to connect to God."

The big lie about God that's currently being perpetuated about God on the Mountain of Religion—that we have to work hard and be good in order to know God—is actually the lie in every major religion. This lie is what is meant to separate Christianity from all other religions. It's advanced by the Religious Spirit and is obviously designed to separate us from any need for the cross and the blood of Jesus. Satan attacks our mind so that we despise a gift.

The difference between the God of the Bible and all other religions is that Jesus Christ is the solid evidence that God was willing to do what we couldn't do for ourselves. He not only created a set of standards to help us individually and collectively see our need for His redemption, but He Himself did exactly what needed to be done in order for us to know Him. That is all He ever really wanted and the reason He created humanity to begin with—to have an intimate relationship with us where we know Him just like He knows us—the real Him and not the one we have wrongly perceived.

Satan has the one basic lie that he repackages in many ways to lead us into the cycle of trying to earn love that has been given freely by a good God. Even Christians fall into this deception. We want so badly to feel like we have value and worth, that we try to behave in a way that makes us feel like God could be happy with us. The truth is, none of us will ever sense the true worth and value that we have from religion. Knowing how loved and valued we are only comes out of relationship, and relationship only comes through what God sent His Son Jesus to do for us. The most healing and freeing thing we can realize is that we already have the very value that we crave. It is given to us long before we awaken to a relationship with Jesus or God, before we even draw our first breath. God sending Jesus for us is the proof of the love and worth we already have in God's eyes—before we ever come to know Him or His ways. The way we learn to act and behave after we come into relationship with Him is meant to be a response, not a requirement, to having been redeemed.

7. HOW THIS LIE ABOUT GOD ON THE MOUNTAIN OF RELIGION PLAYS OUT IN CULTURE

If religion is work and performance, then God is a tyrant and taskmaster who pushes us to carry an impossible workload. When we wrongly perceive Him as a demanding, needy being, we are basically left to respond in one of three ways: try to work hard enough to appease Him, stay bitter and angry with Him for putting us in that position, or, as a subtle form of rebellion against such apparent cruelty, roll over and pretend He doesn't exist. Most who have lived long enough have responded in each way at some point, which has created quite an ongoing, collective turmoil in society.

Every nation across our globe has built into its overall culture our man-made versions of God or religion. No one religion has it right or is perfect, because all are influenced by imperfect people. By the way, that doesn't make God or His heart for us less than perfect. In our collective attempt to navigate our way to God, we establish our own standard of truth based on whatever seems right to us. The problem is that, like everything else, we filter what we think is right through our personal experiences and perceptions of those experiences. Truth, by its very definition, cannot be subjective. It has to be absolute. It is not a feeling or a fad that comes and goes with the whims of whatever generation is presently leading. God is truth, the very standard and unchanging reality that reality is based on, no matter what culture or nation you live in. Religion, like the other primary areas of culture that we are mentioning, is our response to Truth, to God Himself. Religion is not God but rather our response to who we perceive Him to be. Having no religion at all is just as much a response to who we perceive God to be.

8. THE BIG TRUTH ABOUT GOD ON THE MOUNTAIN OF RELIGION: WE NEED A REDEEMER IN ORDER TO KNOW GOD

Holiness is not some part of God that needs us to behave because He likes to be demanding. Let's use the Sun in our sky, for example. Of course, it's made up of fire, and if you got too close to the Sun and were killed by its fire, it would not be because the Sun is mad at you or unfair or unjust. The Sun is what it is, and unless we are like it, if we get close to it, it consumes us simply because of its very essence. In the same way, the holiness and perfection of God is His essence, and whatever is in us that's not like Him is consumed when we draw near to Him. The holiness of God doesn't kill us because God is mad with us but because, by its very nature, it consumes whatever is not holy also. If by faith or simple belief we have not exchanged our sin (the ways we are not like God) for Jesus' perfect ability to do things God's way, then the presence of God that we so desperately want and were created to live in will destroy us. This is why we need another way of access to His heart and to His home—God as our Redeemer. There's a price to pay that only God Himself could pay for us for us to truly be intimate with Him, which is what He has always desired from the ones He created. Only righteous blood could satisfy the need for holiness that can withstand closeness to the One who is holy. So, God the Son willingly came to earth and became man because a human being's sacrifice is what was required for the redemption price of humanity to be satisfied. He willingly gave Himself as the price to be paid so all humans could vicariously have access to God and Heaven. Grace is receiving the favor of God without having to earn it. Truly His grace is amazing because it's what saves us from ourselves and opens our eyes to see how good He really is and how valuable we are to Him. When we stop busying ourselves from either working to earn His love or running from the shame we feel by falling short of trying to earn it, we have that sense that we have finally been found. We don't have to behave perfectly or think perfectly to be made right with God. He expects less than perfection from us. He says that if we will just believe that Jesus sacrificed His life on our behalf, we can be as close to Him as we choose to be and experience true intimacy through God as our Redeemer.

Although we each have our own journey to discovering intimacy with Him, there is only one way to Him, and that is through receiving Jesus, whom He sent to redeem or purchase us back from the deception of the enemy. When you declare Jesus as your Savior, or Redeemer, you are undoing the lies Satan perpetrated against our Father's correct reputation from the beginning of creation. You are coming out of agreement with lies that present Him as less than who He really is. Scripture also tells us that whoever believes in Christ Jesus will not be put to shame, and whoever calls out to Him will be saved from everything we need to be saved from.

9. OUR ASSURANCE ON THE MOUNTAIN OF RELIGION: YOU HAVE ETERNAL SECURITY

When we encounter God as Redeemer, through Jesus, we are assured of our eternal security. Even though we don't deserve it, God has secured a place for each of us forever with Him in heaven. We were valuable to God before we knew our need for Jesus, and because of our value, He sent Jesus to redeem us. As believe in and relate to Jesus as our Savior and Redeemer, He has already dealt with everything that has ever or will ever come between each of us and God. God is capable of redeeming each of us and everything about our lives.

10. PARTNER WITH GOD AS REDEEMER ON THE MOUNTAIN OF RELIGION

To properly fulfill our assignment on the Mountain of Religion we must truly know God as Redeemer ourselves, learn to reflect who He is as Redeemer personally, and then connect it to the way we interact with others. We must become experts on this aspect of God's love and then give it away to all who are influenced by our role on this mountain, remembering that what He made available through Jesus must never be diminished by our obsession with merely trying to get people to behave (wrongly representing God as the same) or by imposing Christianity on others, but rather simply offer Jesus as the gift of unconditional love and acceptance that He is.

NOTES

A REFORMER'S ASSIGNMENT ON THE MOUNTAIN OF RELIGION

1. Become so personally convinced that you don't ever have to work hard and be good in order to know God, that you never feel distant from Him. What you have you can then give away.

2. Know that you have permission to love others extravagantly and radically without having to "seal the deal" of salvation. God never loves anyone with an agenda. He loves because that's who He is, what He does, and what we mean to Him. We can do the same knowing that it carries value in God's eyes. It is the Holy Spirit who draws people to Christ.

3. When you have the opportunity to lead others to Jesus as Savior and Redeemer, connect them to the grace of God and not a wrong perspective of a God who is only concerned about their sin, as if that is an end in itself. He sent Jesus so that we could begin a relationship with Him, not a relationship with religion, rules, or laws.

4. Live grateful and constantly aware of your need for a Redeemer so that when you encounter someone else who appears more lost than you, you aren't tempted to judge them in thought or in the way you interact with them.

5. Have compassion on those who are stuck in idolatry or dead religion. They are living without the provision and protection they were meant to have because they serve a god with empty promises.

6. Have no tolerance for the Spirit of Religion in yourself, while fighting for (not against) those others who have been deceived by it.

7. Understand that the Mountain of Religion can only experience true reformation through the dynamic leading and power of the Holy Spirit. Expect the Spirit to work in unexpected ways and be sensitive to His voice.

8. Live wildly, passionately in love with the Lord and refuse to practice a religion based on platitudes and principles, well-scheduled worship services, and neat and tidy theology. Stay open to supernatural experiences with God that

defy the expectations and traditions of status quo Christianity. Honor Jesus by making room for the Holy Spirit who He sent to help us partner with God in bringing His kingdom to earth.

NOTES

FOR MORE IN-DEPTH INFORMATION ON THESE TOPICS IN OUR OTHER RESOURCES:

The Seven Mountain Prophecy (Ch 9, Overview)

The Seven Mountain Mantle (Ch 18)

The Seven Mountain Mandate Video Course and Workbook (Session 7)

Rainbow God: The Seven Colors of Love (Ch 4)

Rainbow God Video Course and Workbook (Session 6)

The Seven Mountain Renaissance (Ch 5)

GOD AS REDEEMER

My sons and daughters, my heart longs for you to have your security in Me and nothing else. You don't ever need to work hard to be close to Me. Just believe. Believe that I had a plan and that My plan worked. I gave My son, Jesus, to the earth—to doubt, to ridicule, to be betrayed, beaten and crucified just for you. I gave Him to the earth as the only perfect One...to live in righteousness and then be unjustly sentenced to death so that you would never have to live under the reality of your imperfection. Your reality, if you'll believe Me, is this...you are righteous because Jesus made you righteous. You are already perfect because Jesus was perfect enough for the both of you. He's more than enough to resolve anything that has or ever will come between you and Me.

So, stop trying to be perfect. I don't need you to be perfect. You have a Redeemer, One who paid all that you will ever owe, with no strings attached. You choose. Work hard... for nothing, or believe in your Redeemer, Your Savior, Jesus and receive My Kingdom for all of eternity. It is My honor to give it to you! Please don't allow the enemy to add anything to the simplicity of the truth of what Jesus did for you...he has for so long, but through you, I say enough! Enough striving. Enough living like I'm unreasonable and angry with the world. See My compassion, My kindness—and give it away radically and extravagantly.

Know it and live a life of freedom that convinces others of the truth of My heart towards them, the truth of Jesus. Refuse to be preoccupied with sin...your sin, their sin. It's irrelevant in the light of My holiness. You will be holy as I am holy as you look at Me, as you do life with Me, as we process together.

I've wired all of you to grow up into Me as we have relationship. You can't grow up into holiness apart from Me and neither can anyone else. Just look at Me and teach them to do the same. I'm so pleased with even one glimpse from you, from any of My children. I'm not waiting for you to get it together before you turn to Me. Turn to Me now in every way because I made a way for you through your Redeemer—through your Redeemer alone—nothing more and nothing less. He is your way to draw near without your sin consuming you. I want you near Me now, not when you get better or act better. Honor Me by living free from guilt and shame. Honor Me by speaking and acting in a way that convinces others that they too are free from guilt and shame if, and only if, they believe and receive My perfect Son as their Redeemer.

Education is the
most powerful weapon
which you can use
to change the world.

— Nelson Mandela

CHAPTER EIGHT

THE MOUNTAIN OF EDUCATION

In the area of culture referred to as EDUCATION, we see God as TEACHER, the color INDIGO/DEEP BLUE. He is LOVE displayed as WISDOM. This is the wisdom we were meant to grow in through our education experiences. Wisdom is the understanding of when and how to apply facts, truth, and experiences. In order to become wise, we must encounter the wonder and awe of all God has made and set into motion within a safe environment that allows us the freedom to discover for ourselves that all of it points back to Him. God Himself, as Teacher, convinces us that we are far more important than what He is teaching us and, because we are important, He has important things to teach us. Satan uses the principality BEELZEBUB (LIES) and the demonic strategy of the AMORITES (HUMANISM) to distort the truth of who God is. God has given us a mighty archangel, RAZIEL, to fight for those called to this mountain. The LIE being perpetuated about God in our current EDUCATION SYSTEM is: TRUE WISDOM IS SELF DEPENDENCE. The TRUTH that we will learn to display in EDUCATION is: TRUE WISDOM IS DEPENDENCE ON GOD.

1. THE AMORITES AND THE PRINCIPALITY BEELZEBUB: THE DEMONIC STRATEGY ON THE MOUNTAIN OF EDUCATION

The word Amorite means *to say boastfully* and represents the enemy's destructive strategy of humanism on the Mountain of Education.

The AMORITES were one of the seven nations the Israelites had to conquer in order to obey God and take their promised land. They represent the humanism on the Mountain of Education that causes us to believe that everything revolves around us and true wisdom is dependence on ourselves.

BEELZEBUB is Satan's illegal principality on the Mountain of Education. His name means *lord of the flies*. Flies are attracted to rotten food and humanism along with rationalism, agnosticism, and atheism are similarly rotten and poisonous to us and society as well. The demonic strategy was and still is the same—to tempt us to eat of the tree of the knowledge of good and evil, which opens up to all of those ideas that sound intellectually appealing, but their end is death to everything good. Another related demonic influence, the Prince of

Greece, is associated with the humanistic philosophy that was released globally through ancient Greek culture and thought. It was key in collapsing that society from the inside out because its civic outcomes are disastrous. It manifests as left-brain dominant, prideful instruction (similar to the Amorites) and always steers away from God—and by extension away from good. Moral bankruptcy is the direct outcome.

The face of the enemy in education is humanism, but beneath that is fear. Fear leads to humanism, which we have said is basically the belief that since we are alone we must be the center of our own universe and sweat and fight for everything we get. God values dependent effort, but humanism esteems independent effort. Humanism looks like pride, but beneath the pride is a core of fear. That fear instructs us that since we are alone, we had better prop ourselves up with at least a show of self-confidence. The enemy looks to use whatever education system we have in place, whether Christian or not, to enslave the next generation of God's sons and daughters to fear. Fear has many ways it touches students, from anxiety over being accepted to the fear of failure. Where fear is, there is no experience of love, and where there is no love, there is no wisdom (learning and applying what we learn to our future). Fear leaves you in survival mode with no energy left to discover things like your dreams and passions that can help change the world. Where there is no wisdom, no one is really being educated beyond simply memorizing facts.

Beelzebub's Strategy:

1. Prevent the face of God as Teacher from being restored to society.
2. Prevent humanity from having access to the truth of how God loves us through the ways He instructs us in wisdom.
3. Prevent people from knowing that true wisdom is dependence on God, not on yourself.
4. Prevent people from experiencing a healed perspective of the goodness of God through the Mountain of Education, which was ultimately meant to assure us of our importance.

2. THE ARCHANGEL RAZIEL FIGHTS ON THE MOUNTAIN OF EDUCATION

RAZIEL means "secret or secrets of God." — His name reveals His assignment which is to assist in restoring the image of God in the earth as Teacher.

This great archangel who carries the mysteries of heaven and earth is the opposite of the Prince of Greece who has no fresh wisdom or revelation. Raziel and his host of angel armies serve the Lord of Hosts by helping the sons and daughters of God who are called to impact the Mountain of Education. They carry scrolls of wisdom from heaven and are focused on our mission to replace humanistic thought with education that produces people who are ultimately dependent on God. Raziel fights with us to overcome the demonic realm through God's ever-advancing kingdom.

3. THE FACE OF GOD AS TEACHER ON THE MOUNTAIN OF EDUCATION

Habakkuk 2:14 tells us that the end-game is "the knowledge of the glory of God covering the earth." If the end-game is the true knowledge of God, then the entire process is a progressive education.

As we look at the face of God as Teacher we see a God who cares more about us than what He's trying to teach us. In our school systems, we're generally made to feel that the instruction is actually more important than we are. A one-size-fits-all approach is taken and if we don't happen to make that connection, we're flunked. We're just another number and we learn to bend to the system or we're considered failures.

Characteristics of God as Teacher:

1. God as Teacher does have some set rules and principles, but He takes an entirely customized approach to how He teaches His kids. He's aware that He wired us all differently, so He knows how to condition the instruction according to the wiring He has put inside each of us. Every one of us experiences customized education from God the Teacher.

2. God as Teacher is amazingly patient. He can peer into every heart and see who's resisting Him and to what degree—things that teachers here can only guess about. He knows who needs more patience and He knows who needs more immediate consequences. He is perfectly wise—knowing how all aspects of knowledge are to be applied.

3. God as Teacher is completely aware of our natural age and our spiritual age,

and He gives us age-specific lessons. He totally loves loving us through this wise way that He teaches us. He's more of an expert on us than He is on His curriculum. He uses and teaches principles, but He's not in love with His principles. He's in love with us.

4. God as Teacher creates an atmosphere where we, as His students, each feel prioritized, even over the curriculum.

5. God as Teacher builds in rewards for those with a hunger for learning. Scripture speaks of Him as being "the Rewarder of those who diligently seek Him." Proverbs 25:2 says, "It is the glory of God to conceal a thing: but the honor of kings is to search out a matter." This means He likes to hide things and He considers it to be a royal attribute to be curious enough to search for what is hidden.

6. God as Teacher is not boring and predictable, but He rather loves to create an environment where curiosity is awakened.

7. God as Teacher is never focused on just trying to get us to make good grades or pass a test as the end in itself, but rather about adding to our arsenal of knowledge and understanding of Him, His ways, and how to better steward life.

8. God as Teacher instructs us with stories of life itself. Jesus who was called Rabbi or Teacher also demonstrated this aspect of the Godhead. Jesus taught His disciples and the multitudes not with complex charts and sophisticated terminology, but He used what they could relate to and were already familiar with. Parables were His specific methodology for teaching. None of what He taught was just so that His disciples or the people could consider themselves smart or educated. His wisdom is always applicable to real life. Knowledge that has no real application is just vanity and feeds pride.

9. God as Teacher is always instructing and educating us purposefully. All His wisdom starts with the principle that He is the center of everything. Education is meant to be the understanding of how we relate to God and His creation.

10. He loves to be the one that lays out the dots that need to be connected—but He loves us to do the connecting of the dots.

Even though God is the epicenter of every living thing—and this is the core of any real education—there still can be a wise way to educate without imposing God on anyone. We can lay out these dots in curriculum that leads the student to that conclusion as a natural part of their discovery.

4. THE COLOR INDIGO ON THE MOUNTAIN OF EDUCATION

Indigo or dark blue is the color associated with the Mountain of Education. In the rainbow this deep blue indigo transitions into the last color, violet, which connects to government. Our ultimate assignment given to us in Revelation 5 is, "We shall reign on the earth." So, the understanding is that the deep blue is advancing us so much in the knowledge of God's ways, that we are being positioned to receive the government of God on the earth. Deep blue is about insight, wisdom, and revelation, and it's a core aspect of who God is as Teacher.

In chromotherapy, the study and science of healing through colors, blue (connected to religion) has been identified with regulating the circulatory system while the deeper blue color indigo is identified with purifying the circulatory system. Education is like the 2.0 of Religion because it is the practical discipling into what you believe.

5. GOD'S LOVE DISPLAYED AS WISDOM ON THE MOUNTAIN OF EDUCATION

> *"Worthy is the lamb that was slain to receive power*
> *and riches and WISDOM and strength and*
> *honor and glory and blessing."*
> ***Revelation 5:12***

Worthy is the Lamb to receive wisdom! Wisdom is the heavenly attribute associated with the face of God as Teacher. He wants to provide wisdom for us, but then when we connect the dots He has laid out, we will then bless Him in return with the wisdom we've grown in. The Greek word used here for wisdom is *Sophia*. Its definition is "Supreme intelligence such as belongs to God. The wisdom to execute counsels."

The blazing image of God as Teacher will shine on and through us through the Mountain of Education. Wisdom isn't just general knowledge of facts and information. The Holy Spirit is the embodiment of wisdom. He's called the Spirit of Truth, the Counselor, and Comforter. It's Wisdom that instructs us how to advance the reformation of society.

Imagine a child's coloring book with dots on a page that, once connected in the correct order, show a picture that was previously unseen, waiting to be discovered. Wisdom is applied knowledge—the difference between disconnected dots and dots that have been properly connected. As we restore His full face, His many colors, and all His names—God's house on earth is being built. Proverbs 9:1 says, "Wisdom has built her house; she has hewn out her seven pillars." God's house on earth is founded in love, but it's built by wisdom. Love has many faces and it is wisdom that instructs which expression of love to use and even when to use it. Even as a parent raises their children they're aware that love is manifested in different ways. It is out of love we take our kids and buy them an ice cream cone. It's also out of love that we say no more ice cream or sweets today. Out of love we give them permission to go out and play and it's also love that constrains them at times for their protection.

Love works with wisdom as the tour guide. Love is always the appropriate response to any situation, but what facet of love to showcase is not always clear. It's of utmost importance for anyone with an assignment on this Mountain of Education to be a person filled with the Holy Spirit and then to be "continually being filled" as Ephesians 3:19 says.

We have too many "Christian educators" whose wisdom is not the wisdom from above. It's left brain, rational, humanistic wisdom that's straight from the tree of the knowledge of good and evil. That tree champions and prioritizes critical thinking that weighs all the pros and cons of everything. That kind of thinking is a wisdom of sorts, but it conspires against the fruit of the tree of life. The tree of life fruit is being led by the wisdom of the Holy Spirit—often in ways that are counterintuitive to critical thinking processes. God does most of His amazing works in counterintuitive ways. Critical thinking processes will always have you walking outside of faith. Stepping into faith always requires abandonment of the mind of rational wisdom.

It was never wise for Moses to raise his rod and expect the Red Sea to part.

Critical thinking would cause someone to think of that as a ridiculous exercise, yet the Sea parted! True wisdom requires belief that the invisible is greater than the visible. Jesus was the ultimate violator of earthly wisdom. He breaks up one little boy's lunch to feed 5,000 men. He spits on dirt and sticks it on a blind man's eyes. He walks on water. He dies in order to overcome death.

If we want to see the face of God as Teacher and His characteristic of wisdom brightly shining in our education system, we are going to have to be set free from the restraints of this world's wisdom. We have to be people of the Spirit.

6. THE BIG LIE ABOUT GOD ON THE MOUNTAIN OF EDUCATION: TRUE WISDOM IS SELF-DEPENDENCE

Every time we're exposed to the Mountain of Education, the enemy wants our individual and collective takeaway to be, "We're on our own, therefore we need to realize that the only real answers and solutions are within us."

The big lie about God that's currently being perpetuated on the Mountain of Education—that true wisdom is self-dependence—is often exalted as an ideal, but the reality is that it is evidence of an orphan spirit. The enemy hates God so much that he wants us alienated from our Father.

7. HOW THIS LIE ABOUT GOD PLAYS OUT IN CULTURE

When we believe we're the only ones we can truly count on, the loneliness is profound. What begins as a theory becomes our reality. The collective ache is tangible throughout society. Every spare moment and dollar is spent trying to fill the distance we feel from the One we were never made to go through life without. We were not made to strive and scratch for everything we get in life. We were invited into a delightful dependence on a God who is more than enough for everything we don't have enough of. So we scramble and compete our way to our definition of success, wearing ourselves out and stepping on anyone who threatens our pursuit of happiness. Because we don't have any resources other than what we gather ourselves, we protect them at all costs, sometimes even at the expense of what really matters in life. We get an education for the purpose of living for what we can attain in status and material wealth but lose precious relationships, reinforcing the initial lie we were operating out of—that we can only depend on ourselves.

Self-dependence infuses culture through the education system by slowly convincing children that if they don't perform well and compete with their peers academically, their future isn't too hopeful. While it's certainly true that a good education is a big part of preparing for a good job, it definitely isn't a foolproof plan. Being able to memorize, understand, and communicate information doesn't guarantee anything.

Even our next breath isn't guaranteed apart from God. The truth is, you can play the education game perfectly and still end up with a messed-up life. In the end, if your years spent studying do not teach you utter dependence on God, you most likely will stay stuck believing the false concept that your good grades and performance will get you acceptance, approval, and advance in life. That black-and-white, one-size-fits-all form of education promotes competitive, hierarchal, fight-your-way-to-the-top thinking that stays with you the rest of your life. That's knowledge without wisdom—information wrongly applied.

A prevailing flaw in all educational systems is the emphasis on left-brain understanding of truth. Extreme prejudice against right-brain ways of thinking transform the vast majority of children from those who are able to receive creative, imaginative, intuitive revelation from God to those who are rationalistic, critical, and so limited to the five human senses that they can't receive God's revelation. Left-brain based instruction is devoid of elements of faith and trust and champions only that which is observable to the natural eye. For this reason, when Jesus showed up into the Prince of Greece's dominant world that He was born into—He said "Repent, the kingdom of heaven is at hand." This was not a statement to be sorry for their sins, it was rather a statement directing them to change the way they processed things.

The word "repent" comes from a Greek word *metaneo* that means completely shift from one side to another—essentially from left-brain (rational, linear) dominant thinking to right-brain (intuitive, experiential) dominant thinking. This goes into our essential assignment on this mountain. Satan is always trying to alienate or disconnect the Father from His kids. No education of any sort is worth any long-term good at all, if it separates us from the One who is the Source of everything. That's why Proverbs 9:10 says "The fear (reverence) of the Lord is the beginning of wisdom."

8. THE BIG TRUTH ABOUT GOD ON THE MOUNTAIN OF EDUCATION: TRUE WISDOM IS DEPENDENCE ON GOD

If you don't trust God, it's unlikely that you will allow yourself to fall into His arms. It's no surprise to any of us that it's extremely hard to learn to trust God. It's a heart skill that can take a lifetime to grow in. Jesus mastered the concept of dependence on His Father moment by moment. Even though He was the Son of God in bodily form, He looked to God as the Source for everything He needed to know, for all the power He used to heal, and for the strength He needed to trust God with on the path to the cross. When we look at Jesus, we see God as Teacher, among other things.

Healthy learning is not about performing for approval and acceptance and is definitely not meant to happen in an atmosphere of fear and lack of care for the person. People are more important than information. The student getting the education is always more valuable than the education he or she is receiving. God gave us a world to discover because He loves us and wanted to give us more opportunities to know Him and what He is like, not because He planned on leaving us to figure it out ourselves as some survival game He could watch to amuse Himself. Self-dependence creates a climate where people serve knowledge rather than knowledge serving people. Self-dependence makes us wrongly believe that our performance in school secures our future and our ability to survive. In truth, it's God who sustains us and is the source of all wisdom. There's no greater ignorance than the inability to comprehend how absolutely dependent we are on God.

9. OUR ASSURANCE ON THE MOUNTAIN OF EDUCATION: YOU ARE IMPORTANT

When the face of God as Teacher is correctly displayed as Wisdom on the Mountain of Education we are assured of our importance.

God has important things He wants to teach each of us, but they're not more important than we are. He values us and our unique ways of learning and has given us not only an important assignment in life, but He's also capable of preparing us and giving us a clear pathway to get there. When we are dependent on Him we are able to access His solutions for the problems in society.

10. PARTNER WITH GOD AS TEACHER ON THE MOUNTAIN OF EDUCATION

In order to properly fulfill our assignment on the Mountain of Education we must truly know God as Teacher ourselves, learn to reflect who He is as Teacher personally, and then connect it to the way we instruct others and influence our education system. We must become experts on this aspect of God's love and then give it away to all who are influenced by our role on this mountain.

A REFORMER'S ASSIGNMENT ON THE MOUNTAIN OF EDUCATION

1. Do all you can to address obvious problems in schools such as class size, lack of discipline, weak curriculum, etc., but remember these will always be secondary compared to the need to create a proper teacher-student dynamic. Always seek to re-image how God instructs us.

2. Your primary goal in education should be to connect students to their individual passion and the answers to the problems of that area of culture that they are interested in solving. It just so happens that God is the One with those answers, therefore…

3. Restore wisdom the process of educating—the ability to know what to do with what we know.

4. Be careful not to make children feel shuffled through an education system like numbered cattle just to check off the responsibility of having "educated" them. God as Teacher doesn't do that to us. He cares so much about each one that His desire is for them to love learning and discovering truth, while finding their unique passion and gifts.

5. Don't be content to merely teach facts about our world, but help students connect to their potential individual contribution to the world. Only then have they been truly educated.

6. Teach your students that the goal of their education is not to be smart or even position themselves for a successful career. The goal of education is to discover our place in God's world and heart. As we discover our place

in His world, our heart is then able to connect the dots and understand our place in His heart.

7.   Look for new ways to allow more right-brain processing of truth. Create educational experiences that make room for personal learning styles.

8.   Prioritize making students feel like they are even more important than what you're trying to teach them. What they are learning is important only because they are important.

God isn't panicked because we aren't making sure every child knows the Ten Commandments and prays before they eat their lunch. He's so much bigger than that. You have to be told He didn't create everything in order to not believe in God as Creator. Wisdom, in the context of public education, gives the student the essentials for discovery, trusting God to reveal Himself. Ideally, parents are the voice and lifestyle demonstration at home of direct instruction about God.

FOR MORE IN-DEPTH INFORMATION ON THESE TOPICS IN OUR OTHER RESOURCES:

The Seven Mountain Prophecy (Ch 7, Overview)

The Seven Mountain Mantle (Ch 13)

The Seven Mountain Mandate Video Course and Workbook (Session 4)

Rainbow God: The Seven Colors of Love (Ch 7)

Rainbow God Video Course and Workbook (Session 7)

The Seven Mountain Renaissance (Ch 6)

GOD AS TEACHER

My sons and daughters, you know you've found the real Me when you embrace wisdom. You'll know you've embraced wisdom when you mature to the place of utter dependence on Me. You need Me more than you've learned or been taught. Your dependence on Me is the safest place, full of the greatest treasures of knowledge that exist.

My heart towards you, towards humanity, is to freely give you access to all that is life, to all the beauty and mystery of My creation and to all the solutions that I've provided for every effect of sin in your lives and in the earth. I love instructing you because I love you. Because you are important, I have important things to tell you and teach you. In fact, every bit of knowledge that humanity has tapped into, I freely made available to those who had the passion to seek for it.

I've celebrated every aha moment with you and every invention that brought more ease, comfort, and hope. I love it when you discover more of Me hidden around you and in you. I love it when you're curious and adventurous....and I enjoy providing times and places for you to search out My mysteries and delve into things many don't see or won't see.

But don't stop with information, as if it is in and of itself the grandest treasure. Follow the facts into wisdom. Into Me. Peer so closely that you find Me in the micro and train your eye to the vastest horizons and find Me there too in the macro. Enjoy the life I've given you, this time and space, to discover not only Me, but yourself, your assignment. Believe Me when I tell you, you have an important one. It's going to require complete dependence on Me, true wisdom. Show the world how we do it, how we do it together.

There is good government
when those who are near
are made happy, and
when those afar are attracted.

— Confucius

CHAPTER NINE

THE MOUNTAIN OF GOVERNMENT

In the area of culture referred to as GOVERNMENT, we see God as KING, the color PURPLE. He is LOVE displayed as POWER. This is the power that was meant to be seen through a good government. This kind of power is incorrupt authority that exists for the purpose of serving and protecting people's freedoms—which allows citizens to live in a safe environment and have the freedom to discover for themselves who they can be and who God is. This kind of government allows its citizens to believe they can be successful and thrive, not just survive. LUCIFER himself (through PRIDE and MANIPULATION) uses the demonic strategy of the GIRGASHITES (CORRUPTION) to distort the truth of who God is. God has given us a mighty archangel, URIEL, to fight for those called to this mountain. The LIE being perpetuated about God in our current GOVERNMENT SYSTEM is: GOD DOESN'T CARE ABOUT US. The TRUTH about God that we will learn to display in GOVERNMENT is: GOD DOES CARE ABOUT US.

1. THE GIRGASHITES AND LUCIFER:
THE DEMONIC STRATEGY ON THE MOUNTAIN OF GOVERNMENT

The word Girgashite means *dwelling in clay soil* and speaks of the enemy's strategy to invade the Mountain of Government with *corruption*.

The GIRGASHITES were one of the seven nations the Israelites had to conquer in order to obey God and take their promised land. They represent the demons of corruption that operate on the Mountain of Government, as well as the strategy to cause people in governmental positions of authority to become motivated by corrupting influences.

LUCIFER himself is the illegal principality on the Mountain of Government. His name means "light bearing one" and yet he operates through *pride* and *manipulation*. This is seen in many of the secret societies (Illuminati, Masonry, etc.) that attempt to control this mountain. Lucifer was created to be a witness of all that God did and to testify of that to the subsequently created angels. He did that for a season, but that assignment was stripped from him when sin was found in him and he rebelled. He now functions as the anti-light or anti-Christ and from this mountain seeks to hijack God's meta narrative. Satan, formerly Lucifer, parades as light but is just white-washed darkness. He teaches those on this mountain who are susceptible to use bribes and corrupt ambition to advance his agenda of defaming the true nature of God.

Civil wars and chaos have often centered around a nation's quest for a form of government that people want to live under. Essentially every political party and every form of government has at some point been someone's enemy in the war over government. No system or party is perfect because there are no perfect people. The real enemy remains the same as in every area of culture—Satan himself, ruler of the darkness and father of lies. Behind the visible realm of things, a tremendous war is taking place over the governments of the world. Lucifer has understood the all-encompassing power that governments are capable of, so he has assigned himself to embark on the destruction of nations through their own government. In every sphere he has the same objectives. Use the structure itself to steal, kill, and destroy, marring that aspect of who God is in our eyes.

Lucifer's Strategy:

1. Prevent the face of God as King from being restored to society.
2. Prevent humanity from having access to the truth of how God loves us through the way He correctly models His power on the Mountain of Government.
3. Prevent people from knowing that God cares about us through the way He governs.
4. Prevent people from experiencing a healed perspective of the goodness of God through the Mountain of Government, which was ultimately meant to assure us that we are royalty like Him.

2. THE ARCHANGEL URIEL FIGHTS ON THE MOUNTAIN OF GOVERNMENT

URIEL means "Flame or fire of God" — His name reveals His assignment which is to assist in restoring the image of God as King on the earth.

It seems likely that Uriel is actually the angel of Revelation 10:1-3 where it describes "a mighty angel clothed with a cloud…and a rainbow on his head… with his face like the sun and his feet like pillars of fire…he puts his right foot on the sea and his left foot on the land." He may also be the angel of 2 Kings

19:35 who went into the camp of the Assyrians and killed 185,000 in one night by himself. He's a powerful angel! Ultimately Uriel and his host of angel armies serve the Lord of Hosts by helping the sons and daughters of God who are called to impact the Mountain of Government. They are focused on our mission to fill government positions with humble, integrous, servant-hearted, visionary leaders.

3. THE FACE OF GOD AS KING ON THE MOUNTAIN OF GOVERNMENT

When we know God as King we become convinced of His absolute power and authority. He is the Ruler of heaven and earth and has all authority. After the cross Jesus boldly proclaimed in Matthew 28:18, "ALL authority in heaven AND EARTH is mine." He temporarily lost legal authority on earth by means of Adam's sin, but He regained that which was lost through the sacrifice of the perfect sinless blood of Jesus Christ.

Our ultimate assurance that His glorious master plan is going to be realized is because of the overwhelming scale of His omnipotence. He is and has always been all-powerful. He could have chosen or still could choose to be anything He wants. Whereas with humans— absolute power corrupts absolutely—in His case His absolute power has only brought out the deeper veins of the love that is His essence. God as King is complete power, under restraint.

Besides His absolute power making nothing truly impossible, it is His amazing humility and patience that marks His Kingship. His restraint is beyond comprehension which is why we often wrongly expect judgement from Him. We obsess over opportunities or reasons He has to judge people and nations, while He obsesses over opportunities and reasons to pour out His mercy. He is a King fully committed to winning by love and by influence when intimidation and absolute power are fully at His disposal. Our King came as a Servant to all and even His triumphal entry was made on a donkey. In Matthew 21 He announced, "Your King comes to you lowly, riding on a donkey."

Our King is the only royalty whose throne has no walls of privilege or protection built around it. Here on earth only the elite gain access to throne rooms. In heaven, it's open to all. He is the only King that has made the ultimate sacrifice so that all His subjects could have the same level of wealth and privilege that He does. These characteristics of God as King are to be studied and re-imaged into the Mountain of Government. As we do this we literally bring the government of heaven to earth.

4. THE COLOR VIOLET ON THE MOUNTAIN OF GOVERNMENT

Violet is the color connected to the Mountain of Government. Although violet was not originally a color, but rather a flower that was purple, it's the descriptive word for the color purple. Purple is historically associated with royalty, nobility, luxury and power. It is also the rarest naturally occurring color in the rainbow, which is instructive in itself. Too much government is against God's value for freedom.

In chromotherapy, the study and science of healing through colors, it has been identified that too much of the color violet/purple brings out qualities of irritability and arrogance, while too little stirs feelings of powerlessness, neglect, and apathy. Similarly, too much government engenders arrogance and entitlement and not enough government can cause one to feel powerless and neglected. Only our King knows how to govern in just the perfect measure of power.

5. GOD'S LOVE DISPLAYED AS POWER ON THE MOUNTAIN OF GOVERNMENT

"Worthy is the lamb that was slain to receive POWER
and riches and wisdom and strength and
honor and glory and blessing."
Revelation 5:12

Worthy is the lamb to receive power! When we receive and model any of God's seven primary attributes of love we are, in essence, restoring His correct reputation on earth. He receives what we have become and displayed on earth. We are becoming back to God what He has provided for us and through us to others.

God doesn't just love us in theory. His love is expressed in a nuanced way that is unique on each mountain. It is love in action and it expresses His genuine care for us through practical solutions in every area of our lives and our culture. On the Mountain of Government God's love is experienced as power. When love is communicated through governmental systems it registers on the heart of the citizens as power in the perfect balance. The Greek word used here for power is *Dunamis*. This is a word that means "to be possible, can do, force, power, might—with a component of wonderful or miraculous attached to it."

NOTES

Government that is free from corruption releases us to experience the power of love that uses authority for our good, which is why love looks like incorrupt power in the context of governmental authority. Any authority that exists other than for the good of the ones it serves is corrupt. Through government (the seat of authority and power of a nation) we were meant to grow up feeling safe and secure enough to be given the opportunity to be who we want to be. Government and all healthy authority protect the possibility of who we can become. When done well, government communicates to our hearts that we have the opportunity to succeed.

When the ruling authority is abusive and corrupt, the citizens, sometimes generation after generation, get stuck in a cycle of just trying to survive rather than breaking through into true prosperity and destiny. In the same way that each of us exists to fulfill a unique destiny, so too each nation exists to contribute its own special sound and resources to the earth. When government functions the way it is supposed to, love is displayed as power—the power to prosper in every way. Government must exist to create the ability or power for its people to thrive. When it does, it conditions the hearts of those people to believe that God the King is indeed good.

6. THE BIG LIE ABOUT GOD ON THE MOUNTAIN OF GOVERNMENT: GOD DOESN'T CARE ABOUT US

Every time we're exposed to the Mountain of Government, the enemy wants our takeaway to be, "The constant corruption, politics, and issues in government overwhelm me. It seems like every time I have to interact with any government-run system, program, or office I eventually end up feeling like the very people who are called to serve me simply don't care about me at all."

The big lie about God that's currently being perpetuated on the Mountain of Government—that God doesn't care about us—is advanced by the devil because it is the greatest slander against God that there is. Because of our tendency to relate to God in ways culture has related to us, we again find ourselves beset by a very simple but deadly lie. The way most governments presently run leaves us often feeling simultaneously abandoned, exploited, and like we are just another number. That is what the enemy is able to do as he distorts the glory of godly government by bringing it in the wrong spirit and in the wrong measure. God is good, but He is not a micro-manager and He is more about freedom than about order. We will one day be fully aware of this truth when we are in Heaven. The order of heaven is guaranteed by the humility it requires to get into heaven. The freedom of heaven is guaranteed by His image.

Proverbs 29:2 says "When the righteous are in authority the people rejoice; when the wicked rule the people groan." An important assignment on the Mountain of Government becomes to discover what it is that makes the people "groan" and to turn it into something that makes them "rejoice." Following this simple idea helps disassemble the big lie that Satan the accuser wishes to advance through his dominion of this sphere of society. We are wired to connect any kindness done to us as an extension of God's kindness to us.

7. HOW THIS LIE ABOUT GOD PLAYS OUT IN CULTURE

When a nation's government is riddled with scandals and thievery and obviously exists for the benefit of those in power rather than for the ones it serves, the effect on that nation is fear, apathy, and hopelessness because the people see no possibility for prosperity, growth, and change.

When we collectively believe that God doesn't care about us, of course we will simply continue to do things the best way we can and not look to Him for help. And as we've established, God desires intimacy with us and therefore gives us the freedom to choose whether or not to look to Him for what we need. He guards our choice to ask for His help so that when we do look to Him, it comes from a sincere heart and desire for Him and His better ways. His desire for real relationship with us is greater than the risk He takes of us believing awful lies about Him like this one. We reap the consequences of this core belief that God does not care about us in our systems of government.

When corruption abounds in the government of a nation, the citizens end up being enslaved to poverty because the leaders don't allow the money and resources to go where they are most needed. The pride and corruption of those in authority serve their own agenda and do not have the good of the people as their motivation. They may talk as if they care for the poor, but the proof will be in the overall prosperity of the people in the context of each area of culture—family, religion, media, education, economy, and arts/entertainment. The collective heart and soul of nations bound by their government's corruption feel as if they are behind the rest of the world, tired of hoping for change, and ultimately abandoned by God Himself. Apathy and misery settle upon generation after generation, and soon the people can't remember ever feeling cared for by the leaders they look to or loved by God. You can know that you suffer because of the choices of evil men, but at the core of every hurting heart is the haunting question of why God does not intervene. We reason that if God is God and He is good, then He should be powerful and good enough to make the evil stop. He should be able to stop the corruption that keeps us back and holds us down.

God deals with the hearts of nations as He does with our hearts individually. He is not content to simply deliver us from sin but also wants us to really live and be free in every area of our hearts and lives. Similarly, God is not content to simply deliver our nations from corruption, but He also wants to deliver them from anything that keeps us from knowing the real Him. He wants the citizens of nations free from the effects of corruption, so they can know Him and His heart for them—so that they can know that He cares. He understands that when we thrive under healthy government, we are more likely to believe that He cares about us.

8. THE BIG TRUTH ABOUT GOD ON THE MOUNTAIN OF GOVERNMENT: GOD DOES CARE ABOUT US

When we start with the assumption that God does care about us and that He is the Almighty, can-do-anything God, then we realize that we only need to discover *what* that solution is, and not *if* there's a solution. There is always a solution to any and every problem when God the King is invited in. It's impossible to bring before God something that He considers a quandary. Answers and solutions naturally spill out of His identity as King. Doing the impossible is His norm. Whether the solutions disappoint some of the people in the short run, they'll all see—in the long run—the wisdom, justice, and compassion of His strategic solutions.

There are no public political debates over laws that are outside God's jurisdiction of insight and power. For example, He knows how to address the homosexual debate with so much wisdom that no one feels uncared for. He knows how to project and promote into policy the right wording that simultaneously watches over the supreme right of freedom of individual choice, as well as protect the overall population from any general moral decline in society.

If we are to be involved in governmental reformation, we really must understand His great value for personal freedoms. Our "Christian" tendency is usually towards order—which focuses on outside-in pressures and restraints—

while God's tendency is towards freedom, which is an inside-out restraint. Adam and Eve were put in a garden with a "do not touch" tree at their disposal, because it was important to Him that their choices of righteousness be given along with the freedom to choose wrongly.

He runs government with a freedom to choose wrongly. We must provide the freedom to choose wrongly when that freedom will not directly affect any other. No society is conclusively headed for judgment from God, just because they allow their people certain freedoms such as marrying the wrong person or watching bad movies. These are all trees of the knowledge of good and evil options in society that reveal actual hearts, as opposed to perceived righteousness. True righteousness always takes place in the context of free will. Of course, freedoms that clearly infringe on another person's freedom do need to be curtailed.

The kingdom of God does not advance through compulsion, and that was pointedly revealed to us through the person of Jesus. He could have showed up with 10,000 angels of war and intimidated the whole of society to fall in line and obey every whisper He made—but He isn't after subordination at any cost. He's after winning hearts who then freely choose His ways. A properly run government steers a heart towards God without imposing God on anyone. Therefore, it cannot be an oppressive police-state type government and simultaneously reflect the way God governs. Our God truly cares for every one of His citizens on earth, and He's fully capable and empowered to heal any and every natural crisis that emerges.

Many ask why He allows horrible suffering around the world? He is asking us, why have we allowed starvation and suffering, etc.? He's ready to reveal His solutions, but first we must care because we believe He cares. Then we must access His power because we believe He has power for solving all government related issues. We must come out of agreement with the lie that God doesn't care about us.

We must invite Him in, and where He's acknowledged governmentally, He will come in and show His awesome care.

9. OUR ASSURANCE ON THE MOUNTAIN OF GOVERNMENT: YOU ARE ROYALTY

When the face of God as King is correctly displayed as Power on the Mountain of Government it assures us that we are royalty.

God cares about each of us and none of us are just another person on earth that He has to tolerate. His throne is not only approachable, but we belong next to Him, and He is able to make us ready to rule and reign with Him as His children filled with love for Him and His kingdom. He's protective over each of us and our freedom. He is just and merciful. Our King is maintaining an atmosphere around us that we can thrive in, not simply survive in.

10. PARTNER WITH GOD AS KING ON THE MOUNTAIN OF GOVERNMENT

In order to properly fulfill our assignment on the Mountain of Government we must truly know God as King ourselves, learn to reflect who He is as King personally by the way we embrace our own royalty, and then connect it to the way we serve and lead. We must become experts on this aspect of God's love and then give it away to all who are influenced by our role on this mountain.

A REFORMER'S ASSIGNMENT ON THE MOUNTAIN OF GOVERNMENT

1. Be firmly established in the assumption of God's power and greatness, as well as the fact that He cares about every injustice in our lives.

2. Know that the problems you face in the context of your role in government are indeed too big for you, therefore assume you will need and be able to access the King's solutions. A government that's run by people who see Him as King will pass on to its constituents a healed perspective of God that relaxes nerves and gives peace. Conversely, a government that is bent on proving they can figure everything out—because God is in fact not on the job—will be one that passes on anxiety to its constituents.

3. Remember that when we're talking about reflecting God's power in government, it's the power of love. Love must be restored to government, and more importantly to the hearts of those who govern. We can't give away what we don't have. It's difficult to display an authority motivated by love when we haven't submitted to an authority over us that is motivated by love. When we come under the power of love, we will lead with the power of love.

4. Don't claim your identity as a Christian as part of your credentials to govern or serve. Allow your life actions and the position of your heart to

speak for itself. Many people are afraid of Christians because they believe we're going to try to force people into our way of relating to God. History unfortunately has fueled this fear by events such as the Crusades and the various Inquisitions.

5. Ultimately, if you carry authority in government you were meant to have authority over the darkness that steals freedom from people, but not over people themselves. There's a fine line between the two. The King we serve is protective over our right to choose Him and His kingdom because when we choose, He wants it to be sincere and not forced. He dominates over the things that keep us from choosing Him, willingly restraining His power to dominate over us. Anyone who does not rule in the same way is ruling in a form of corruption. We aren't created to dominate or rule over people but over Satan and principalities. Ruling, in its truest sense, is serving.

6. Refuse to participate in bribery, corruption, or control through manipulation.

7. Ask God to deal with pride in you that may tempt you to abuse the authority you've been trusted with.

8. Connect your thinking and your platform to values, not ideals. Connecting to ideals alone won't hold anyone in the intense and treacherous battlefield of politics. Most politicians start out with ideals, but compromise comes easily to those whose values are separated from the God behind the values.

FOR MORE IN-DEPTH INFORMATION ON THESE TOPICS IN OUR OTHER RESOURCES:

The Seven Mountain Prophecy (Ch 6, Overview)
The Seven Mountain Mantle (Ch 12)
The Seven Mountain Mandate Video Course and Workbook (Session 2)
Rainbow God: The Seven Colors of Love (Ch 5)
Rainbow God Video Course and Workbook (Session 8)
The Seven Mountain Renaissance (Ch 8)

GOD AS KING

My sons and daughters, kings and queens in training on the way to the throne. In order to understand my kingdom and my government, you must know that your experience with earthly government is quite inferior to Mine. My kingdom is the context in which My heart, as your King, is seen. As your King, I'm delighted to serve you. I'm delighted to share My power with you and display to and through you My better ways of doing everything.

I created you with royalty in your veins, whether you ever feel it or not. I created you to know Me so well that you care about what I care about. You are an extension of Me and My kingdom in the earth. You are proof that I rule and reign with wisdom and mercy and justice. My government, the way I do things as an extension of My very heart towards humanity and creation—My government, was set into motion before time. And what I set into motion always only ever increases.

My kingdom, My government is always only ever increasing. If you have eyes to see, the kingdom has come and is coming like a runaway train that cannot be stopped. It's coming in you, around you, and through you and all who are Mine.

Open your eyes, open their eyes to the good news—My kingdom is overtaking your lesser, deficient ways of doing things. Believe and tell them...Orphans no longer! Sons and daughters! Together, we shall reign on the earth. We will reign over all sickness, over all disease. We will reign together over poverty and lack. We will reign together over every injustice and over every broken system.

You and I—we will reign over every lie that has ever been told or even implied about who I am and who you are to Me.

CHAPTER TEN

THE RISING REFORMERS

*"**Arise**, shine, for **your** light has come!*
*The glory of the Lord is **risen** upon **you**.*
The darkness will cover the earth and deep darkness over the people,
*but the Lord will **arise** over **you** and His glory will be seen upon **you**.*
*Nations will come to **your** light*
*and kings to the brightness of **your rising**!"*
Isaiah 60:1-3

The mission of reformers is to arise and shine with the light and knowledge of both *who* God is and *how* He is in every mountain of culture in every nation. The discovery of who God is in *us* and what parts of His image *we* were uniquely designed to carry is a search and journey all in itself. Most Christians express having a lot of doubt as to exactly what their assignment is. The seven-mountain message has been useful in helping many people identify a mountain they're passionate about, which then clarifies their assignment. You'll also find that it provides fresh language for the things God's already been doing in you and through you.

You've received revelation and understanding of the seven mountains, how to recognize the lies about God in each area of culture, what truths to replace them with, and ultimately how to partner with God in restoring the fullness of who He is to society. Realistically, you won't be prepared to accomplish any of this until you apply those same dynamics personally. In the same way we have described the battlefield in culture, we are all personally assaulted with lies and must fight for the truth in our own hearts and minds daily.

Because our own identity is so connected to who we perceive God to be, all lies we're tempted to believe about *ourselves* are ultimately about *God*. All personal truths to fight for are ultimately about God. There's one big lie that Satan is constantly bombarding everyone with: Your life doesn't really matter. It's important to recognize that this is the basic lie the devil is feeding all of us. To accomplish this task, He has assigned demons to tell us that. He also strategically uses the broken-down state of culture, and especially the areas of culture you're passionate about, to reinforce the lie in every way possible.

To be a reformer of culture and not just one who is conformed to society, we must first be personally set free from the lies that take us out. Again, it's very difficult to give away that which you don't have yourself. So, your personal lie to deal with as a reformer called to arise and shine is: My life doesn't really matter. You may not be consciously in-touch with that feeling, nor depressed over it. Your brain may be fully aware that your life definitely matters, but in the sometimes mundane and sometimes difficult trials, is your soul fully convinced? People who really aren't sure that they matter treat themselves, others, and even God as if *they* don't really matter. If you don't think your life really matters, you may feel momentarily inspired by a message like this but remain in a mode of wandering without real purpose to each day. We've all been there at times—reacting to whatever comes next, rather than focusing, following through, and responding to God's invitation to more.

There's yet another lie behind that lie. Remember, every lie (even the ones about you or others) is in reality a lie about God. If you believe you don't matter, then a central lie will be that God can't possibly make every person matter—He seems to have too many people to care for and too many things to do. The truth is God is not too busy for us and He isn't even 1% anxious with the challenges of all the problems of the universe and the rebellious demons. So yes, He has time for **you** to matter. We think, "How can everybody matter? There are billions of people on the planet. Not every person can be important and make a difference. Somebody has to just be the normal person and it's probably me." Wrong! The truth is everyone is wired in God's image and His image always matters. His image always carries purpose. If we can't be convinced of that for ourselves, then how are we going to convince the world of that truth?

There is no mistake, handicap, defect, marital status, educational status, etc. that can keep you from imparting something of great value to the world. God took the time to wire you in a unique way, fully knowing every challenge you would be born into, every choice you would make, and every subsequent challenge you would face. He attached purpose to everything He breathed into—even if it's hard to discover. Reformation starts with you. It's impossible for you not to be important.

The dictionary defines a reformer as "a person who makes changes to something so as to improve it." Are you ready to be improved? Are you ready to improve those things that you're passionate about in the world around you? God is ready for your yes.

If you're going to be a reformer, you'll need to know and embrace the core values of a reformer:

1. Every person is a son or daughter of God, although some don't yet know or acknowledge it.

2. This isn't a get-it-done, knock-it-out, conquer the world kind of assignment. It's a relational assignment where we overflow with the love we've been given by God.

3. God loves us unconditionally and gives us permission to do the same with others.

4. Our love, like His, must be expressed in action and in practical solutions to real life problems.

5. Our care, like His, must be authentic and not out of obligation, performance, or hidden agenda.

6. Our worship is more than a song. It's a lifestyle that overflows to others.

7. Our value for others, like His, must not be based on our differences or someone's awareness of their need for Jesus. We were valuable to God before we ever knew we needed Him and others are too.

8. People are innately wired to experience real love as the real God, therefore we don't feel pressure to connect the dots for them when we are being kind. We understand that people are prone to feel God's love when something goes right for them, even if they don't notice it consciously in the moment. God respects people's process, so I can too.

9. It's not enough to pray for the mountains of culture. We must actually show up and serve. Prayer is good, but we must occupy the areas where we want to see change.

10. Israel has a crucial role in the end-times and we must acknowledge that and align ourselves with God's honor for the firstborn among His many nations.

11. God actively seeks for opportunities to show mercy rather than judgement, therefore we will too.

12. God is more concerned about our stance on someone's heart than He is concerned about our stance on their sin. It is the Holy Spirit that leads us into conviction and His kindness that leads us to repentance.

13. Our unconditional love may at times appear that we are condoning sin and that's ok. Love hitting it's intended mark is more important.

14. We can seek to make new progress in the reformation of society while still validating and honoring progress that's been made in the past.

15. No matter how different our opinions and perspectives are from God's, He always listens to us and makes us feel heard. We must do the same for others.

16. We focus on things we have in common with others rather than what we may not have in common.

17. We acknowledge the talents and breakthroughs anyone has contributed to culture in a positive way as being from God, even if they don't acknowledge God as their source. Every good and perfect gift comes from Him and we can help heal someone's perspective of God when we celebrate and help them understand that the thing they are passionate about is actually Him.

18. There is nothing that cannot be redeemed by God, so our privilege is to maintain a hopeful perspective about everyone, every situation, and every nation.

If you're going to be a reformer, you'll also need to know which one of the four primary roles you are called to serve in. All are equally valid and important to reformation.

Protagonist — one who has the typical job description on the mountain (such as a teacher on the Mountain of Education).

Advisor to Protagonist — one who advises another on the mountain (such as an advisor to a politician on the Mountain of Government).

Intercessor to Protagonist — one who is anointed to intercede for someone with a role on the mountain.

Financier of Protagonist — one who funds someone with a role or a project on the Mountain.

No matter what role you take as a reformer on your mountain, a key point is not to fret about the defective systems that are there. You can waste a lot of time and lose a lot of resolve trying to get rid of what is faulty or broken or trying to convince others of the need for change. Instead, ask God for revelation and insight as to an upgraded system, strategy, or initiative from heaven. It will sell itself. Steve Jobs and Apple didn't need to strategize against the old phone with cords or oversized mobile phones that we all had at one time. There was no point starting a campaign against what was the status quo. There is no real sense in getting rid of something unless there is something better. The only thing needed was the discovery of an upgraded model. Smartphones with their present convenience and capacities easily made the other phones laughable relics.

The best days are ahead, and we have many decades of kingdom advancement right before us. We are going to know God like we have never known Him before. Nothing is impossible at a personal level, at a family level, at a church level, at a city level, or at a national level. No matter what your situation, no matter what's happening in your nation—ALL THINGS ARE POSSIBLE. We have known the God of salvation and now we are going to also know the God of solvation. The only impossible thing is to find something impossible for Him. Creative solutions and advanced innovations overflow from who He is. As He is in this world, so are we. Let's seize the day, seize the hour, and seize the moment. Let's live on fire with who He is—the One blazing with seven flames of fire. Worthy is the Lamb to receive the reward of His sufferings. Let's RISE and give Him the nations.

There is no greater pursuit than to see and know our God in a more intimate way. Discover Him and champion Him. May the insight you've received from the seven-mountain message serve as a personal catalyst to help you become further enraptured by who He is and what He's doing and will do in the earth through reformers like you. Be convinced of His hope-filled storyline and run to find your place in it. Heaven on earth awaits your participation. God thought of you in eternity and caused you to be born on earth in this generation for such a time as this. No matter what your color, age, gender, level of education, amount of wealth, or status in life, God has given you something with which you can shine in a reflection of His glory. You've been given something specific that can be used to bring fame to God on earth and to display the truth about how good He is. There is some nuanced knowledge of *who* He is and *how* He is that you were designed to shine with. May you discover His glory that was meant to be seen on you as you RISE!

What's Next?

Download the RISE app
Join the RISE Global Community

Reformers are those who are ready to walk in their purpose outside of the four walls of the church. They are waging war on religion and on the mindsets that have caused God's reputation on earth to be less than He really is. These reformers love radically without religion's agenda and believe the goodness of God can be expressed in every area of culture: Media, Family, Arts & Entertainment, Economy, Religion, Education, and Government.

RISE, which stands for Reformers Influencing Society Everyday, is the answer for lovers of Jesus who know they were created to change the world, but haven't known exactly what that looks like in real life. God desires to partner with His sons and daughters to display the truth of not just who He is, but how He is in the earth and reform every broken system in the seven mountains of culture.

If you're fully convinced that the real God loves the world and has solutions for every problem that exists in society, then RISE is for you. By reading the RISE handbook or by completing the RISE Course online, you'll be ready to join the RISE Global Community.

By reading this RISE handbook OR by completing the RISE Course online, you qualify to join the RISE Global Community. Simply join by installing the RISE app on your device. When prompted, use the following code as proof of completion of this handbook: X73ZP2542WWS

To learn more: www.RESTORE7.org.

KNOW THAT I LOVE YOU

You are My daughter. You are My son. I love you. You belong to Me. Oh, what delight I have that you are Mine! What delight you give Me when you know that you're Mine! You are hidden in Me and nothing can take you from My hand. Nothing can divert My gaze from being on you. It always has been and always will be. Today and tomorrow and through every night. You are always in my sight.

I am yours. I am in you. I hold you together in the very structure of who you are. I hold you. I surround you. You have access to all of Who I am, from close, from within you. I am behind every breath and every beat of your heart. I know you in ways you can't even imagine or understand. I know everything about you...what makes you, you. I know your every thought, word, choice and action. I know you so well that I know what you'll do and the choices you'll make before you even make them, because I know how you're made, what you've been through, and how you've processed things.

You don't overwhelm me, and I'm never discouraged when I think of you. I know you...and I love you. I'm easily able to enjoy you like you are, right now.

You're one that I have chosen before I set time into motion. I chose you to live now. I chose you to come alive to the reality of Who I am in this time in history. I chose you because I wanted you to know Me like I know you. I wanted you to discover, in a way that you'll know for all of eternity, that I value you. I wanted you to discover that I want you. You matter. You have significance because I made you, because you are My son... because you are My daughter.

I want you near Me with nothing between us. Jesus, His perfection, was enough to tear down anything that would ever keep us apart. Because of your great value to Me, I sent My very best just for you. Before time, I created you perfect and blameless, enough to fill My heart with joy forever. What was stolen from you, from us, has been restored! I look at you and see you as I made you—perfect! You don't disappoint me—you thrill my heart with one look My way!

I am for you. I was for you before you were born. I was for you in the midst of the lies of your circumstances and tragedies and crisis. I was for you in your worst moments so far. I was for you yesterday and I will be for you tomorrow. I will be for you every moment you have yet to experience. I'm already there waiting for you—waiting to show you Who I am and how much I care. You must look for Me... I'll be the One for you. I'll be the One with the answers you're looking for, the peace you're craving, the love you're needing. I'll be the One cheering for you. I'll be the One speaking life to sustain you and comfort you. I'll be the voice of truth, so listen for Me. I'll be the proud Papa waiting for you to come home to—always ready to process with—the One

NOTES

with the satisfied look on My face, full of pride in who you are because you're Mine.

I tell you now, and every day, if you'll hear Me—you are of immeasurable worth to Me. You have value beyond your comprehension. Anything that tells you otherwise is a lie from our enemy.

You matter. I've given you important things to say and important things to do because you are important. So, say them and do them boldly and in confidence, as one who is valued, loved, and important—because you are. Do them with Me and through Me—because all I've ever really wanted was to be close to you and for us to know each other face to face.

In Me, you can do anything. You can get through anything. You can be as important as I created you to be! I value you so much that I want you to represent Me. Show them who you know Me to be. You can know Me... you already do more than you think you do. You've seen Me, and you've known Me, and You can know Me in an ever-increasing way.

Discover Me today. Look for Me—and care about what I care about. Know Me. Know that I love you. No one could love you more than I do right now. I am your Papa, your Rainbow God, your seven colors of love.

APPENDIX

OVERCOMING END-TIMES-ITIS

By Johnny Enlow

Perhaps nothing has been more sabotaging to the Body of Christ's assignment to be salt and light and thus transforming society then what I call the virus of end-times-itis—a "condition" marked by the expectation of soon-coming, end-of-world scenarios.

Endtimesitis involves believing that either the rapture, or Jesus' return, or a one-world government, or the anti-Christ, or Armageddon or some whole list of cataclysmic judgments is right around the corner. This "virus" saps our resolve and allows fear to reign. It's so widespread among Christians of all denominations (and even among virtually all false religions), that many of you reading this right now might be taken aback at me pointing this out as an issue. Our goal is to provide some needed truth serum that will vaccinate you from succumbing to it.

This fascination with the end-times has been alive and well among Christians for almost 2,000 years. There hasn't been even one generation that wasn't preoccupied with it. It clearly explains why, despite Christians being the greatest majority on the planet, we have comparatively little influence. It's hard to "arise and shine" when you're secretly, or not so secretly, planning your exit strategy.

I grew up surrounded by Endtimesitis and formerly had the virus. I remember being so sure at age 13 that the signs of Jesus' soon return were clearly there and I would never even get a chance to get married. I'm so glad that wasn't true. In an effort to provide some truth serum to stem this virus, I'd like to explain some of its history over the last 2,000 years. Please know that by naming the people I do, it does not discredit them from being true and sincere servants of the Lord. My own godly father was sure he would see the return of Jesus in his lifetime and he passed on in 2005. His being wrong didn't make him a bad guy, though he did not publicly prophesy this as far as I know. What is more troubling is that some of the names I will mention are known for no other ministry other than speculating on the end times and making millions doing so. I leave that in the hands of God and may He be the judge.

A History of Endtimesitis

1. PAUL, THE APOSTLE: I will controversially perhaps begin with Paul. It is clear through multiple passages that he thought he would see the return of Jesus in his day. In his famous "rapture scripture" of 1 Thessalonians 4:17 the fact that he stated "WE which are alive and

remain will be caught up together with Him…" tells us that he might have expected to be a part of that. It seems that what his spirit was picking up was the destruction of Jerusalem and perhaps his own martyrdom. 2 Thessalonians 2:1-2 gives us insight that this was all a widespread topic of conversation even in his day. "Now brethren, concerning the coming of our Lord Jesus Christ and our gathering to Him we ask you not to be soon shaken in mind or troubled…". Through this we suspect that Endtimesitis was already a problem in Paul's day.

2. CLEMENT OF ROME: After Peter and Paul were martyred it was Clement who became the bishop of Rome. In 90 AD he spoke and said that it was "any day" now when Jesus would return. It did not happen.

3. AUGUSTINE OF HIPPO: (354-430 AD) Famous church leader who strongly influenced Western Christianity and Western Philosophy. Prophesied that Jesus would definitely return by 650 AD. He was wrong.

4. IRAENEOUS: (130-202 AD) Famous early church theologian prophesied along with two other well known Christians leaders that Jesus would be returning in 500 AD. One of them used the dimensions of Noah's Ark as his template. They were wrong.

5. 1000 AD: Multiple ministers and the Pope prophesied end-of-days scenarios. There were riots in Europe associated with it and pilgrims heading to Jerusalem. Wrong.

6. 1005-1006 AD: There was a terrible famine in Europe that was in a widespread way seen as a definitive sign of the end. It wasn't.

7. POPE INNOCENT III: For years spoke apocalyptic language hoping to generate a 5th Crusade to capture Jerusalem. He said the end would come in 1284 AD at exactly 666 years after the founding of Islam, which he said was the antichrist. He was wrong.

8. 1033 AD: Many who prophesied the 1000 AD end adjusted it to this year based on it being 1000 years after Jesus death instead of 1000 years after His birth. Widespread apocalyptic fever. They were wrong.

9. 1346 AD: The Black Plague took out about a third of Europe and this was seen as a "definitive" sign of the end. Ironically the religious fervor of the day caused the Christians to kill all cats as familiars with witches—which caused an abundance of rats which spread the plague. They were tragically wrong.

10. CHRISTOPHER COLUMBUS: Had a book of prophecies and based on careful research predicted the end of the world by 1656 AD. He discovered that he was wrong.

11. MELCHIOR HOFFMAN: Influential church leader. Announced that Jesus would return in 1533 AD exactly 1500 years after His execution and set up the New Jerusalem in Strasburg, Germany. He was wrong.

12. JOHANNES STOFFLER: German mathematician/astronomer. In 1499 announced that based on unique planetary conjunctions that Feb. 20, 1524 a vast flood would engulf the world. He had over 100 endorsements from pamphlets from other leaders. When it didn't happen there were riots and hundreds of deaths.

13. MARTIN LUTHER: Famous Protestant Reformer said the end of the world could be no later than 1600 AD. He then had another date that came and went. He too was wrong.

14. JOHN NAPIER: Famed Mathematician, studied Revelation and said the end would come in 1688 AD, and then revised to 1700 when it did not. Wrong again.

15. JOHN WESLEY, JOHN CALVIN, JOHN KNOX and JOHN WYCLIFFE all had dates come and go for when the end had to be. There's something about the name JOHN and the end times.

16. COTTON MATHER: Famed American Puritan Minster who wrote 450 books and tracts, graduated from Harvard, and was a pastor by age 16 he prophesied 1697, 1716, 1717, and then 1736 as dates for the end. It didn't happen.

17. 1666 AD: Great fear among European Christians as the 1665 plague had wiped out much of London, and then The Great Fire of London came and destroyed 13,200 homes, 87 churches including St. Paul's Cathedral. With it being a year that ended in 666 most were convinced it was the end. It wasn't.

18. 1669 AD: Old Believers in Russia believed the end was that year and so 20,000 burned themselves to death to protect from the antichrist. Zealous, but tragic and wrong.

19. MARY BATEMAN: Not previously famous, but in 1806 caused an uproar as she had a hen that laid eggs that said, "Christ is coming." It was discovered that she was etching the eggs and putting them back in the oviduct and calling people to see them laid. Wrong on so many levels.

20. JONATHAN EDWARDS: Famed Great Awakening Preacher had dates come and go for the start of the millennium.

21. MOTHER SHIPTON: Famed mystic said she was shown the end of the world would be in 1881. Her influence was great, but she was wrong.

22. 1910 AD HALLEY'S COMET: New York Times reported that noted French astronomer Camille Flammarion believed that the comet "would impregnate the atmosphere and possibly snuff out all life on the planet." People rushed to purchase gas masks and "comet pills." Chicago was especially under total fear. Atlanta Constitution reported of safe rooms being prepared and even key holes being covered. After the fact, Chicago Tribune headline was "We're Still Here."

23. JEHOVAH'S WITNESSES: Had 1914, 1915, 1918, 1920, 1925, 1945 as dates for Armageddon and Christ's return. Wrong.

24. WILLIAM MILLER: Founder of the Adventists had an initial date of March 21, 1844, for Jesus' return and then several others after that. Jesus didn't come.

25. HERBERT ARMSTRONG: Founder of Worldwide Church of God said the rapture would take place in 1936. He then changed the dates three subsequent times.

26. HAL LINDSEY: Managed to rev up the Endtimesitis to a whole other level with his 1970 best-selling book *The Late Great Planet Earth*. We and it are still here.

27. TIM LAHAYE and JERRY JENKINS: Essentially rehashed Hal Lindsey's book into a fiction series called *Left Behind* that sold 65 million books and became a motion picture. We are still here.

28. CHUCK SMITH: Founder of Calvary Chapel prophesied 1981 was the time for end time scenarios. He was wrong.

29. PAT ROBERTSON: Charismatic leader prophesied end of world scenarios for 1982 that have not happened.

30. LESTER SUMRALL: Great Pentecostal leader wrote a book *I Predict 1985* for when Jesus would return. He later had an *I Predict 2000* book but that too was wrong.

31. JACK VAN IMPE: Has been prophesying end times scenarios since at least the 1970's. The great tribulation was to have started in 2001 by last reckoning I saw.

32. JOHN GRIBBIN AND STEPHEN PLAGEMANN: Wrote best-selling book *The Jupiter Effect* warning that on March 10, 1982 an alignment of planets on the same side of the sun would trigger a series of cosmic events culminating in an earthquake along the San Andreas Fault that would wipe out Los Angeles. The date came, and the Los Angeles Griffith Observatory was flooded with phone calls. The book had also been endorsed by Hal Lindsey. A year later author wrote *Jupiter Effect Reconsidered* and it too was a best seller thus proving Endtimesitis is an irrational disease.

33. 1919: Albert Porta a meteorologist predicted that during December of 1919 an enormous sun spot would destroy the earth duet electro-magnetic pull on the sun by a rare alignment of Mercury, Venus, Mars, Jupiter, Saturn and Neptune. It didn't happen.

34. RICHARD NOONE: In the 1990's wrote a book titled *5/5/2000: Ice-The Ultimate Disaster* that predicted the polar ice caps melting and submerging large parts of the earth because Mercury, Venus, Mars, Jupiter and Saturn would align with earth for the first time in 6000 years. He was wrong.

35. EDGAR WHISENANT: Retired NASA engineer wrote a book *88 Reasons Why the Rapture Will Be in 1988* based on crunched numerical clues. It sold millions. When 1988 passed he revised it to 1989 and still sold a lot of books. He then changed to 1990, then 1992, then 1993. We with Endtimesitis are quite the suckers.

36. GARY BLEVINS: Author who wrote *666: The Final Warning* in 1998, said that Ronald Reagan will be cast into the lake of fire, the rapture will occur, Jesus will return, Satan will be bound 1000 years. He was wrong.

37. HAROLD CAMPING: American broadcaster and evangelist first came out with a end times scenario for 1994, but did not stop when that was not fulfilled. Kept coming up with new books and new dates with the final one having the church raptured May 21, 2011. He made millions with his books and then spent millions trying to warn the world of what was coming. He was wrong many times.

38. 2000 AD: The Y2K computer glitch was predicted by most prophetic voices to push us into end times scenarios. It did not.

39. JONATHAN CAHN: Author, has sold millions of books stating, "the die has been cast" and the formal end to Christian America is upon us. He jumped on the "blood moon" bandwagon but scenarios did not play out as prophesied. He is wrong and especially wrong about America.

40. JOHN HAGEE AND MARK BILTZ: Released books declaring the tetrad of blood moons mark the end times being upon us. They sold millions of books. They are wrong.

If it seems I'm being redundant it's because it is necessary to exterminate this virus so that we will commit to a process of receiving the kingdom of God on earth. The names listed, and the dates given, are in no way exhaustive, but they do cover essentially the 2,000-year timeline I gave. I could have also added Charles Wesley who set a date that didn't come about. Mormon founder Joseph Smith who heard an audible voice giving him a date. Ellen White of the Adventists who was visited by an angel and given a date. Then there is Nostradamus who has as a last possible date 1999. Edgar Cayce missed dates. Perhaps many of you remember the widely reported Mayan Prophecy that had it all ending 12/12 of 2012. The beat goes on and on. Endtimesitis has been pervasive for a long, long time.

Perhaps the greatest present drawback in the unending yearly speculation is that it is complicit with chasing the next generation out of church. They aren't just leaving because they're carnal, faithless, or messed up. They are leaving because they were wired for extreme world makeover and almost no one in the church is speaking into it.

If someone won't stop speaking "end times" scenarios because they're doctrinally convinced not to, perhaps they will do so for the sake of the next generation.

It is amazing that Jesus would say in Matthew 24:36 that no one knows the day or hour, not even the angels, NOT EVEN THE SON, and yet—every generation has somebody trying to disprove that. Furthermore, He has already told us in Acts 3:21 that Jesus is held in the heavens from even coming back until we see the restoration of all things the prophets said we would first be a part of. Are we closer than ever to the return of Christ? Well, yes, but barely, as we have wasted time speculating and fear mongering when we could have been on our seven mountains assignment. The good news is that our God is amazingly patient. He has passed on hundreds of opportunities to fall in line with someone else's time line so that He could stick with His.

His time line will always be more connected to our growth than to Him looking at a calendar or a watch. One of the reasons I'm very sure He's not coming back too soon is because we are still not known for our love. That is not the type of Bride He wants to present to His Son. It makes for bad romance. The good news is we can accelerate things as we suffocate Endtimesitis and embrace His narrative of going after nations with His seven beautiful colors of love. That's what we are to RISE and shine with.

RISE QUICK REFERENCE CHART ....

THE 7 MOUNTAINS	MEDIA	FAMILY	ARTS & ENTERTAINMENT
ENEMY ON THE MOUNTAIN	HITTITES (REPRESENT FEAR)	JEBUSITES (REPRESENT REJECTION)	HIVITES (REPRESENT COMPROMISE)
PRINCIPALITY ON THE MOUNTAIN	APOLLYON (DESTROYER)	BAAL (PERVERSION)	JEZEBEL (SEDUCTION)
ARCHANGEL OF THE MOUNTAIN	GABRIEL (MESSENGER OF GOD)	RAPHAEL (GOD HEALS)	JEHUDIEL (THE GLORY GOES TO GOD)
FACE OF GOD AS	COMMUNICATOR	PAPA	CREATOR
THE 7 COLORS OF LOVE	RED	ORANGE	YELLOW
GOD'S LOVE DISPLAYED AS .... (REV. 5:12)	BLESSING	STRENGTH	GLORY
THE LIE BEING PERPETUATED ABOUT GOD	GOD DOESN'T HAVE A GOOD PLAN FOR US.	GOD HAS ABANDONED AND REJECTED US.	GOD DOESN'T WANT US TO HAVE FUN.
THE TRUTH ABOUT GOD	GOD HAS A GOOD PLAN FOR US.	GOD HAS NOT ABANDONED OR REJECTED US.	GOD WANTS US TO ENJOY LIFE.
YOUR ASSURANCE	YOU HAVE A DESTINY.	YOU ARE ACCEPTED.	YOU ARE ENJOYED.

.... FOR THE SEVEN MOUNTAINS

ECONOMY	RELIGION	EDUCATION	GOVERNMENT
CANAANITES (REPRESENT LOVE OF MONEY)	PERIZZITES (REPRESENT IDOLATRY)	AMORITES (REPRESENT HUMANISM)	GIRGASHITES (REPRESENT CORRUPTION)
MAMMON (GREED)	RELIGIOUS SPIRIT (FALSE WORSHIP)	BEELZEBUB (LIES)	LUCIFER (PRIDE AND MANIPULATION)
ZERACHIEL (PROVIDED BY GOD)	MICHAEL (WHO IS LIKE GOD?)	RAZIEL (SECRETS OF GOD)	URIEL (FLAME OF GOD)
PROVIDER	REDEEMER	TEACHER	KING
GREEN	BLUE	INDIGO (DEEP BLUE)	VIOLET (PURPLE)
RICHES	HONOR	WISDOM	POWER
IT'S POINTLESS TO TRUST GOD FOR RESOURCES.	WE HAVE TO WORK HARD AND BE GOOD IN ORDER TO KNOW GOD.	TRUE WISDOM IS SELF DEPENDENCE.	GOD DOESN'T CARE ABOUT US.
GOD ENJOYS PROVIDING FOR US AND THROUGH US.	WE NEED A REDEEMER IN ORDER TO KNOW GOD.	TRUE WISDOM IS DEPENDENCE ON GOD.	GOD CARES ABOUT US.
YOU ARE PROVIDED FOR.	YOU HAVE ETERNAL SECURITY.	YOU ARE IMPORTANT.	YOU ARE ROYALTY.

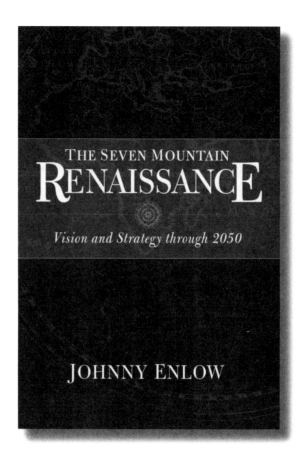

The Seven Mountain Renaissance: Vision and Strategy Through 2050

In *The Seven Mountain Renaissance*, the book we recommend to follow-up RISE, you'll discover a refreshing new perspective of the changing times we live in—an era of kingdom advancement that will be history's greatest renaissance. Where the first renaissance was all about man advancing, this time it's all about the knowledge of God filling the earth through His sons and daughters in every area of culture. Johnny Enlow challenges the reader to see America's spiritual and historical foundation in a way that helps clarify what our mission must be in restoring God's correct reputation to society. This book, filled with rich revelation, is a must read for Christians who want to have a voice of love regarding the latest hot topics in our generation, without compromising truth.

Purchase this book or a PDF download at
www.RESTORE7.org

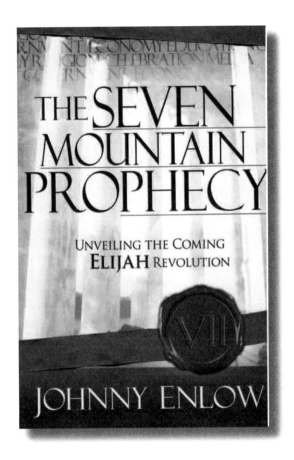

The Seven Mountain Prophecy: Unveiling the Coming Elijah Revolution

The Seven Mountain Prophecy is the first book Johnny Enlow wrote about the seven mountains. It is both prophecy and strategy for the assignment that awaits the sons and daughters of God— to impact not only individual hearts, but also entire cities and nations with the truth of how good God is. Many are awakening to the heart of our Father displayed in Jesus' prayer, "On earth as it is in heaven." You'll discover a fresh perspective on what is required of us in order to see God's kingdom come through our personal lives. The same God that has the answer to our need for a Savior is also inviting us to access His answers for every problem in society. If you've been sensing a need to be challenged into a new way of thinking about the future and your role in it, this is it.

Purchase this book or a PDF download at
www.RESTORE7.org

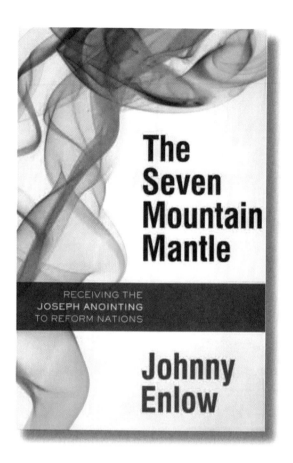

The Seven Mountain Mantle: Receiving the Joseph Anointing to Reform Nations

God is looking for willing sons and daughters upon which He may bestow a mantle of favor that will take them to the tops of the mountains of societal influence. After establishing the criteria for becoming a Joseph, Johnny Enlow then steps into prophetically declaring just what that favor will look like on the seven mountains of government, media, education, economy, religion, family and arts and entertainment. *The Seven Mountain Mantle* will leave you infused with hope and excitement over the amazing things that God is doing among the nations.

Purchase this book or a PDF download at
www.RESTORE7.org

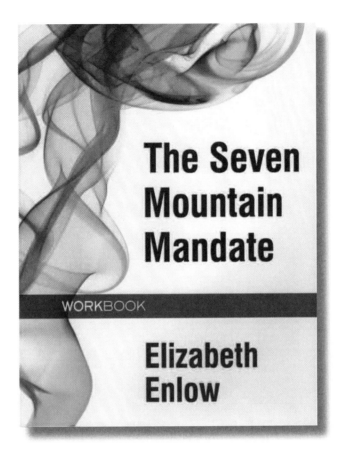

Mandate Video Course and Workbook

In this 9-session video series by Johnny Enlow, you'll be inspired and challenged to function in the fullness of our destiny, specifically in the areas of your personal interests and passions. You'll discover that the very things that you may already be doing in life are opportunities for you to know more of God and therefore display more of Him to the world. Johnny goes in depth on proper end time theology that will give you a fresh perspective on the future as well as personal direction for how you fit into God's plans of restoring His true name, face, and reputation to all. This is a great series to consider for small groups, classes, and anyone who wants to be launched fully into our Father's supernatural solutions that are available for those who want to know Him and see Him revealed on every mountain of society.

Access this free video course on the Johnny and Elizabeth Enlow Youtube Channel. Download the accompanying fill-in-the-blank and discussion/activation workbook on their website bookstore: www.RESTORE7.org

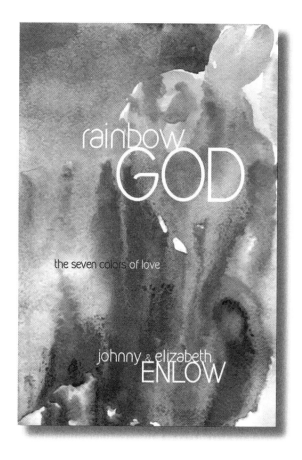

Rainbow God:
The Seven Colors of Love

What comes to mind when you think of God? If you've ever thought of Him as distant . . . irrelevant to culture . . boring . . . uninterested in your passions . . . well, He isn't who you thought He was. There are a lot of lies about Him in this world, even in the church. Whether you're a lifelong believer or hardly ever given Him much thought, *Rainbow God,* co-authored by Johnny and Elizabeth Enlow, will expand your perspective of God. This particular book is a more relationally based understanding of the seven mountain mandate and will give you a fresh perspective of how your journey with God is connected to your unique purpose and life assignment.

Audiobook available.
Purchase this book or a pdf download at
www.RESTORE7.org

Rainbow God Course and Workbook

In this 9-session video series by Johnny and Elizabeth Enlow you'll experience an in-depth process of expanding your perspective of not only who God is, but how He is. Throughout the sessions you'll encounter the seven primary faces of God as Communicator, Papa, Creator, Provider, Redeemer, Teacher and King in a personal way that will equip you to impact the areas of culture that you are passionate about. You'll be encouraged to discover potential lies you may have believed about God and yourself and the truth that will position you to have the influence you were created to have.

Access this free video course on the Johnny and Elizabeth Enlow Youtube Channel. Purchase or download the accompanying fill-in-the-blank and discussion/activation workbook on their website bookstore: www.RESTORE7.org

GOD IN EVERY SEASON
— ELIZABETH ENLOW —

God in Every Season

The cycles or seasons of life that we go through aren't simply an organizational system put into place by a distant God to help us earthlings keep track of time. The seasons you personally go through, and the one you're currently in, are the very backdrop on the stage of the greatest love story of all…yours. The various seasons of your soul are your assurance that not only is your journey with God real, but your story isn't over yet. God Himself escorts you through the changing seasons, makes sure you don't get stuck, and gets the last word on everything that concerns you, because He cares about you. Seasons are an expression of His intimate intentionality to keep you moving forward, progressing, and growing in the knowledge of Him and His true heart for you, beyond the unpredictable challenges and victories that arise. *God in Every Season,* by Elizabeth Enlow, will help you understand which season you're currently in and how to navigate through it with no regrets. This book includes a short questionnaire you can take that reveals the current season of your soul. Through the wisdom and insight she's learned to walk in, as well as her transparent, raw and honest way of communicating, you'll experience an unforgettable encounter with God.

Audiobook available.

Purchase this book or a pdf download at
www.RESTORE7.org

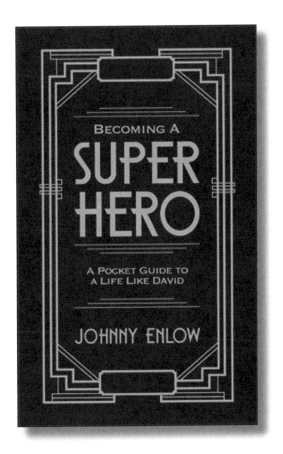

Superhero:
A Pocket Guide to a Life Like David

This book by Johnny Enlow is an easy read, yet full of profound and unique insights into the life of David. By overcoming the personal lies of rejection and insignificance that could have easily held him back, David was prepared to deal with Goliath through the supernatural powers of God within him. Just like David, God wants to help you overcome all that hinders you from discovering the superhero that lives in you.

Audiobook available.
Purchase this book or a pdf download at
www.RESTORE7.org